KU-391-987

GOOD HOUSEKEEPING

MICROWAVE COOKERY MADE EASY

Speed of cooking is the most obvious reason for having a microwave oven. With this in mind this book has been written to help today's cook successfully prepare meals in minutes. The cooking techniques are straightforward and simple, with clear step-by-step illustrations, to help all cooks master the magic of microwave cooking. We include family favourites, such as Roast Chicken, cooked microwave style, as well as more exotic recipes such as Sole and Spinach Roulades suitable for dinner parties. So, whatever the occasion, you will be able to find something delicious to cook among this selection.

With the compliments of

Cookery Notes

Follow either metric or imperial measures for the recipes in this book as they are not interchangeable. Sets of spoon measures are available in both metric and imperial size to give accurate measurement of small quantities. All spoon measures are level unless otherwise stated. When measuring milk we have used the exact conversion of 568 ml (1 pint).

* * Size 2 eggs should be used except when otherwise stated.
* † Granulated sugar is used unless otherwise stated.
* ● Plain flour is used unless otherwise stated.

Bowl sizes
Small bowl = about 900 ml (1½ pints)
Medium bowl = about 2.3 litres (4 pints)
Large bowl = about 3.4 litres (6 pints)

Covering
Cook, uncovered, unless otherwise stated. At the time of going to press, it has been recommended by the Ministry of Agriculture, Fisheries and Food that the use of cling film should be avoided in microwave cooking. When a recipe requires you to cover the container, either cover with a lid or a plate.

HOW TO USE THE RECIPES IN THIS BOOK WITH YOUR COOKER SETTINGS

In this book, the microwave power levels and cooking times refer to a 600–700 watt cooker.

HIGH refers to 100% full power output of 600–700 watts.
MEDIUM refers to 60% of full power.
LOW refers to 35% of full power.

If your cooker power output is lower than 600 watts, then you must allow a longer cooking time for all the recipes in this book.

Add approximately 10–15 seconds per minute for a 500 watt cooker and 15–20 seconds per minute for a 400 watt cooker. No matter what the wattage of your cooker is, you should always check food before the end of cooking time, to ensure it does not get overcooked. Don't forget to allow for standing time.

KEY TO SYMBOLS

*1.00** Indicates minimum preparation and cooking times in hours and minutes. They do not include prepared items in the list of ingredients; calculated times apply only to the method. An asterisk * indicates extra time should be allowed, so check the note below symbols.

Chef's hats indicate degree of difficulty of a recipe: no hat means it is straightforward; one hat slightly more complicated; two hats indicates that it is for more advanced cooks.

£ Indicates a recipe which is good value for money; £ £ indicates an expensive recipe. No £ sign indicates an inexpensive recipe.

✳ Indicates that a recipe will freeze. If there is no symbol, the recipe is unsuitable for freezing. An asterisk * indicates special freezer instructions so check the note immediately below the symbols.

309 cals Indicates calories per serving, including any suggestions (e.g. cream, to serve) given in the ingredients.

Illustrated on the cover: Lamb with Aubergine and Mint (page 27)

GOOD HOUSEKEEPING

MICROWAVE COOKERY MADE EASY

Contents

WATERZOOI

0.20 £ 225 cals

Serves 6

15 ml (1 tbsp) vegetable oil

2.5 ml (½ tsp) ground cloves

2 celery sticks, trimmed and chopped

2 leeks, trimmed and sliced

2 large carrots, peeled and thinly sliced

1 bouquet garni

2 strips of lemon rind

600 ml (1 pint) boiling fish or vegetable stock

700 g (1½ lb) freshwater fish fillets, such as bream, carp, pike or eel, skinned

salt and freshly ground pepper

2 egg yolks

150 ml (¼ pint) milk

6 slices of toast

30 ml (2 tbsp) chopped fresh parsley

1 Put the oil, cloves, celery, leeks, carrots, bouquet garni, lemon rind and half the stock in a large bowl. Cover and cook on HIGH for 12–14 minutes or until the vegetables are softened. Meanwhile, cut the fish into bite-sized pieces.

2 Add the fish, remaining stock and salt and pepper to taste to the soup. Re-cover and cook on HIGH for 6–7 minutes until cooked.

3 Meanwhile, blend the egg yolks and milk together. When the fish is cooked, spoon a little of the liquid on to the egg yolk mixture and mix together. Pour back into the soup.

4 Re-cover and cook on MEDIUM for 1–2 minutes or until thickened, stirring once; do not allow the soup to boil or it will curdle. Discard the lemon rind and bouquet garni.

5 To serve, place the toast in six soup bowls, carefully spoon over the soup and garnish with chopped parsley. Serve immediately.

JAPANESE CLEAR SOUP WITH PRAWNS

0.30 £ £ 105 cals

Serves 4

15 g (½ oz) dried seaweed, such as kombu, wakame or nori

15 ml (1 tbsp) soy sauce

4 raw jumbo prawns in the shell

2 medium carrots, peeled

5 cm (2 inch) piece of daikon radish, peeled

15 ml (1 tbsp) sake or dry sherry

4 slices of lime

1 Put the seaweed, soy sauce and 900 ml (1½ pints) boiling water into a large bowl. Cover and cook on HIGH for 3 minutes or until the water returns to the boil, then continue cooking for a further 5 minutes.

2 Meanwhile, remove the shells from the prawns, leaving the tail intact. Then, using kitchen scissors or a sharp knife, cut along the curved underside of the prawn from the thick end towards the tail, stopping at the tail and being careful not to cut the prawn through completely.

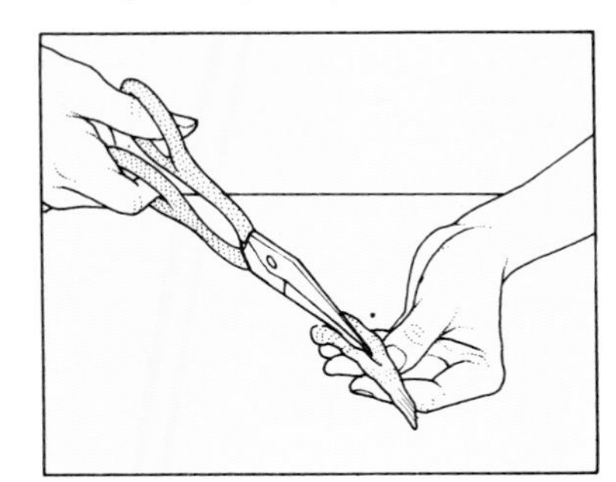

3 Flatten out the prawns and remove and discard the veins. Cut a slit in the middle of the prawn, curl the tail round and push it through the slit.

4 Cut the carrots and daikon radish into thin slices or decorative shapes.

5 Remove and discard the seaweed from the stock. Stir the sake, carrots and daikon radish into the stock. Cover and cook on HIGH for 3 minutes, then add the prawns and cook for 2 minutes or until cooked.

6 Using a slotted spoon, transfer the fish and vegetables to four soup bowls, then carefully pour over the stock. Add a slice of lime to each bowl and serve immediately.

CHILLED PEA AND MINT SOUP

0.35* £ ✳ 224 cals

* plus $2\frac{1}{2}$–$3\frac{1}{2}$ hours cooling and chilling

Serves 6

50 g (2 oz) butter or margarine

1 medium onion, skinned and coarsely chopped

450 g (1 lb) frozen peas

568 ml (1 pint) milk

600 ml (1 pint) chicken stock

2 large mint sprigs

pinch of caster sugar

salt and freshly ground pepper

150 ml ($\frac{1}{4}$ pint) natural yogurt

mint sprigs, to garnish

1 Put the butter into a large bowl and cook on HIGH for 45 seconds or until the butter melts.

2 Add the onion, cover the bowl and cook on HIGH for 5–7 minutes or until the onion is soft.

3 Add the peas, milk, stock, 2 mint sprigs and sugar. Recover and cook on HIGH for about 8 minutes or until the liquid is boiling. Reduce the setting to LOW and cook for 15 minutes or until the peas are really tender. Season well with salt and pepper and cool slightly.

4 Remove about 45 ml (3 tbsp) peas from the soup and put them aside for the garnish. Rub the remaining peas through a sieve, or liquidise them in a blender or food processor until quite smooth.

5 Pour the purée into a large serving bowl. Adjust the seasoning and leave to cool for 30 minutes. Stir in the yogurt and cover and chill for 2–3 hours before serving. Serve garnished with the reserved peas and mint sprigs.

CHILLED COURGETTE MOUSSE WITH SAFFRON SAUCE

0.30* £ 95 cals

* plus 1 hour chilling

Serves 2

275 g (10 oz) small courgettes, trimmed
15 g ($\frac{1}{2}$ oz) butter or margarine
7.5 ml ($1\frac{1}{2}$ tsp) lemon juice
100 g (4 oz) low fat soft cheese
salt and freshly ground pepper
5 ml (1 tsp) gelatine
45 ml (3 tbsp) natural yogurt
pinch of saffron strands
1 egg yolk
fresh herb sprigs, to garnish

1 Cut one of the courgettes into very thin slices lengthways, using a potato peeler or sharp knife. Put the slices into a medium bowl with 30 ml (2 tbsp) water.

2 Cover and cook on HIGH for 2–3 minutes or until the slices are just tender, stirring once. Drain and dry with absorbent kitchen paper.

3 Use the courgettes slices to line 2 oiled 150 ml ($\frac{1}{4}$ pint) ramekin dishes. Set aside while making the filling.

4 Finely chop the remaining courgettes and put into a medium bowl with half of the butter and the lemon juice.

5 Cover and cook on HIGH for 5–6 minutes or until tender, stirring occasionally.

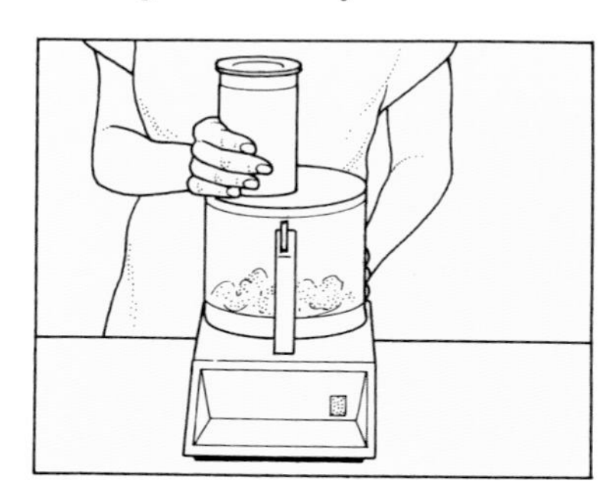

6 Allow to cool slightly, then liquidise in a blender or food processor with the remaining butter and the cheese until smooth. Season well with salt and pepper.

7 Put the gelatine and 15 ml (1 tbsp) water into a small bowl or cup and cook on LOW for $1-1\frac{1}{2}$ minutes or until the gelatine has dissolved, stirring occasionally. Add to the courgette purée and mix together thoroughly.

8 Pour into the lined dishes and leave to cool. Chill for at least 1 hour or until set.

9 Meanwhile, make the sauce. Put the yogurt, saffron, egg yolk, salt and pepper into a small bowl and cook on LOW for $1-1\frac{1}{2}$ minutes, or until slightly thickened, stirring frequently. Strain, then leave to cool.

10 To serve, loosen the courgette moulds with a palette knife then turn out on to two individual serving plates. Pour over the sauce, garnish with a herb sprig and serve immediately.

TINY CHEESE TRIANGLES

0.40 £ ✳ 290 cals

Serves 4

75 g (3 oz) cream cheese
15 ml (1 tbsp) lemon or lime juice
1 spring onion, trimmed and finely chopped
25 g (1 oz) chopped dried apricots or dates
salt and freshly ground pepper
75 g (3 oz) butter or margarine, cut into small pieces
4 sheets of packet filo pastry, thawed
75 ml (5 tbsp) natural yogurt
15 ml (1 tbsp) lemon juice
$\frac{1}{4}$ cucumber
mint sprigs, to garnish

1 To make the filling, mix the cream cheese and lemon or lime juice with the spring onion and chopped fruit and season to taste with salt and pepper.

2 Put the butter or margarine in a small bowl and cook on HIGH for 2 minutes or until melted.

3 Lay one sheet of pastry on top of a second sheet and cut widthways into six double layer 7.5 cm (3 inch) strips. Repeat with the remaining two sheets of pastry.

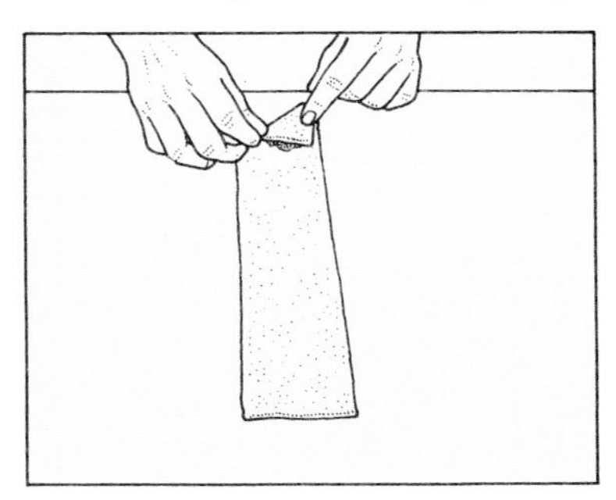

4 Brush the strips of pastry with the melted butter or margarine. Place a generous teaspoonful of filling at one end of each strip. Fold the pastry diagonally across the filling to form a triangle.

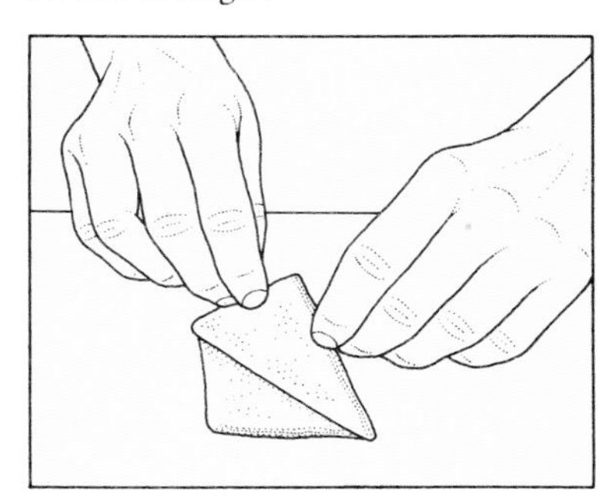

5 Continue folding, keeping the triangle shape, until you reach the end of the strip of pastry. Repeat with the remaining strips of pastry to make a total of 12 triangles.

6 Heat a browning dish on HIGH for 5–8 minutes or according to the manufacturer's instructions.

7 Meanwhile, brush both sides of each triangle with the melted butter or margarine.

8 Using tongs, quickly add six triangles to the dish and cook on HIGH for 1–2 minutes until the underside of each triangle is golden brown and the top looks puffy. Turn over and cook on HIGH for 1–2 minutes until the second side is golden brown.

9 Reheat the browning dish on HIGH for 2–3 minutes, then repeat with the remaining triangles.

10 While the filo triangles are cooking, make the sauce. Put the yogurt and lemon juice in a bowl and mix together. Grate in the cucumber and season to taste with salt and pepper.

11 Serve the filo triangles warm or cold, garnished with mint sprigs, with the sauce handed round separately.

FILO PASTRY

Filo pastry, sometimes spelt phyllo, is a paper-thin pastry made of flour and water. It is possible to make it at home but it is a time-consuming task because of the amount of rolling and stretching needed to make it really thin, so buy it ready prepared and keep it in the freezer until required.

Coarse Herb and Mushroom Pâté

0.15* | 62–83 cals

* plus 1 hour chilling

Serves 6–8

25 g (1 oz) butter or margarine

1 garlic clove, skinned and crushed

2 juniper berries, crushed

700 g ($1\frac{1}{2}$ lb) mushrooms, roughly chopped

75 g (3 oz) fresh brown breadcrumbs

60 ml (4 tbsp) chopped fresh mixed herbs

lemon juice

salt and freshly ground pepper

fresh herbs, to garnish

1 Put the butter or margarine, garlic and juniper berries in a large bowl and cook on HIGH for 1 minute.

2 Add the mushrooms and cook on HIGH for 10–12 minutes or until the mushrooms are really soft and most of the liquid has evaporated, stirring frequently.

3 Add the breadcrumbs and herbs and season to taste with lemon juice and salt and pepper. Beat thoroughly together, then turn into a serving dish. Cover and chill before serving garnished with fresh herbs.

STUFFED PLAICE TIMBALES WITH LEMON HERB BUTTER

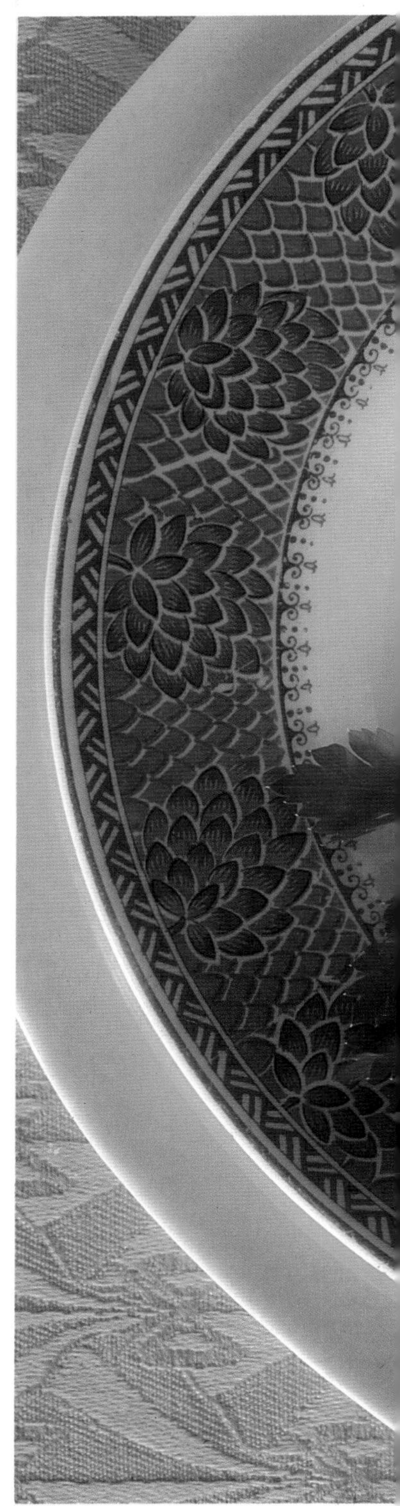

0.25 | £ | 190 cals

Serves 4

25 g (1 oz) butter
5 ml (1 tsp) lemon juice
30 ml (2 tbsp) chopped fresh parsley
salt and freshly ground pepper
175 g (6 oz) mushrooms
15 ml (1 tbsp) vegetable oil
75 g (3 oz) long grain white rice
300 ml ($\frac{1}{2}$ pint) hot chicken stock
2 large double plaice fillets, skinned or 1 plaice, filleted
parsley sprigs, to garnish

1 To make the lemon herb butter, put the butter in a small bowl and beat until soft. Add the lemon juice, half of the parsley and season well with salt and pepper. Beat together well. Push to the side of the bowl to form a small pat and chill while making the timbales.

2 Finely chop the mushrooms and put in a medium bowl with the oil. Cover and cook on HIGH for 2–3 minutes or until the mushrooms are softened.

3 Stir in the rice and the stock, re-cover and cook on HIGH for 10–12 minutes or until the rice is tender and the stock absorbed, stirring occasionally.

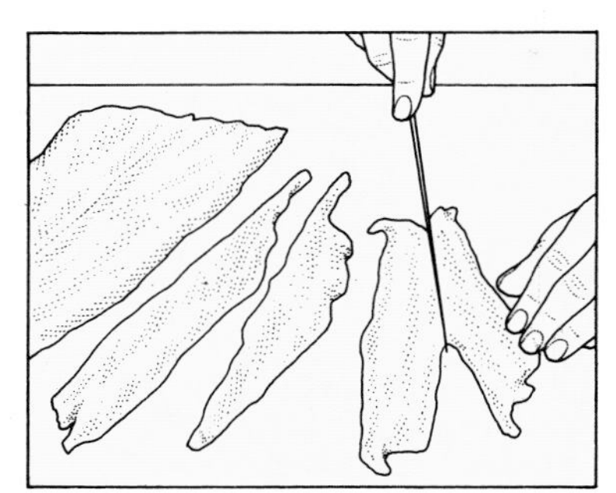

4 Meanwhile, cut the plaice fillets in half lengthways, to make two long fillets from each. Place one fillet, skinned side in, around the inside of each of four buttered 150 ml ($\frac{1}{4}$ pint) ramekin or individual soufflé dishes. The fish should line the dish leaving a hole in the centre.

5 When the rice is cooked, stir in the remaining parsley and salt and pepper to taste. Spoon this mixture into the centre of each ramekin, pressing down well. Cover loosely with absorbent kitchen paper and cook on HIGH for 2–3 minutes or until the fish is cooked.

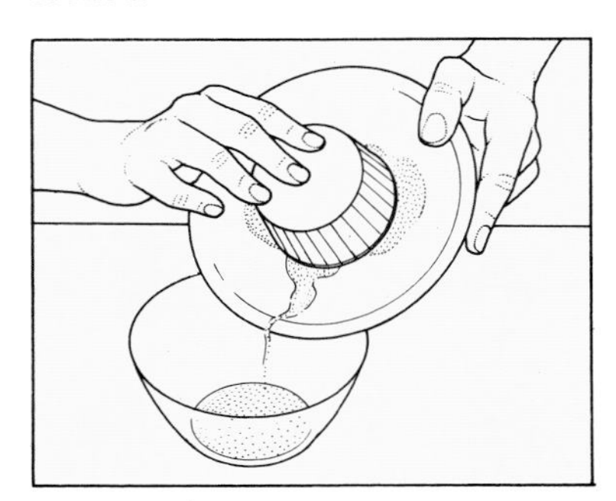

6 Leave to stand for 2–3 minutes, then invert the ramekin dishes on to serving plates. With the dishes still in place pour off any excess liquid, then carefully remove the dishes.

7 Garnish the timbales with parsley sprigs, then serve hot, with a knob of the lemon herb butter on top of each.

Potted Shrimps

0.05* £ ✳ 408 cals

* plus 1 hour chilling

Serves 4

200 g (7 oz) butter

175 g (6 oz) cooked shrimps, peeled

pinch of ground mace

pinch of cayenne pepper

pinch of ground nutmeg

salt and freshly ground pepper

bay leaves and peppercorns, to garnish

1 Cut half of the butter into small pieces, put into a medium bowl and cook on HIGH for 1–2 minutes until melted.

2 Add the shrimps, mace, cayenne pepper, nutmeg, salt and plenty of pepper. Stir to coat the shrimps in the butter, then cook on LOW for 2–3 minutes until the shrimps are hot, stirring occasionally. Do not allow the mixture to boil. Pour into four ramekin dishes or small pots.

3 Cut the remaining butter into small pieces, put into a small bowl and cook on HIGH for 1–2 minutes until melted. Leave to stand for a few minutes to let the salt and sediment settle, then carefully spoon the clarified butter over the shrimps to cover completely. Garnish with bay leaves and peppercorns, leave until set, then chill in the refrigerator before serving.

4 Serve straight from the pots with brown bread and lemon wedges, or turn out and arrange on individual plates.

BRIE AND WATERCRESS TARTS

0.30 £ ✱ 512 cals

Serves 4 as a starter or light meal

100 g (4 oz) plain wholemeal flour
salt and freshly ground pepper
75 g (3 oz) butter or margarine
2 bunches watercress
275 g (10 oz) ripe Brie
45 ml (3 tbsp) double cream
freshly grated nutmeg

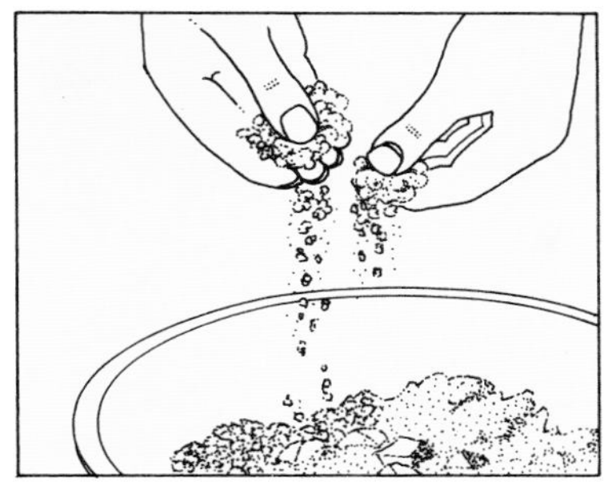

1 To make the pastry, put the flour and salt to taste in a bowl. Add 50 g (2 oz) of the butter or margarine and rub in until the mixture resembles fine breadcrumbs. Add 30–60 ml (2–4 tbsp) water and mix together using a round-bladed knife. Knead lightly to give a firm, smooth dough.

2 Roll out the dough thinly. Invert four 10 cm (4 inch) shallow glass flan dishes and cover the bases and sides with the dough. Cover and chill while making the filling.

3 Put the remaining butter or margarine in a medium bowl and cook on HIGH for 1 minute or until melted. Trim and discard the tough stalks from the watercress. Reserve a few sprigs to garnish and stir the remainder into the butter. Cook on HIGH for 1–2 minutes until just wilted.

4 Remove the rind from the cheese and cut into small pieces. Stir into the watercress with the cream. Cook on HIGH for 1–2 minutes until melted. Season to taste with nutmeg, salt and pepper.

5 To cook the tarts, uncover and prick all over with a fork. Arrange pastry side uppermost in a circle in the cooker and cook on HIGH for 2–3 minutes or until firm to the touch.

6 Leave to stand for 5 minutes, then carefully loosen around the edge and invert on to a large serving plate. Fill with the filling and cook on HIGH for 2–3 minutes or until warmed through. Garnish with watercress.

CREAMY SCRAMBLED EGG WITH SMOKED SALMON

0.06 | £ £ | 844 cals

Serves 1

25 g (1 oz) smoked salmon trimmings

2 eggs, size 2

30 ml (2 tbsp) double cream or milk

25 g (1 oz) butter

salt and freshly ground pepper

buttered toast, to serve

chopped fresh parsley, to garnish

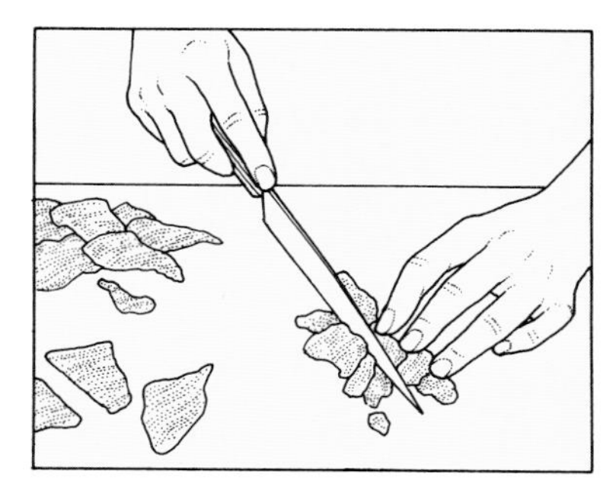

1 Cut the salmon into small pieces and set aside. Then put the eggs, cream and butter into a medium bowl and season with a little salt and lots of pepper. Whisk together well.

2 Cook on HIGH for 1 minute or until the mixture just begins to set around the edge of the bowl. Whisk vigorously to incorporate the set egg mixture.

3 Add the smoked salmon and cook on HIGH for $1\frac{1}{2}$–2 minutes, whisking every 30 seconds and taking care not to break up the salmon, until the eggs are just set but still very soft.

4 Check the seasoning, and spoon on to the toast. Garnish with chopped parsley and serve immediately.

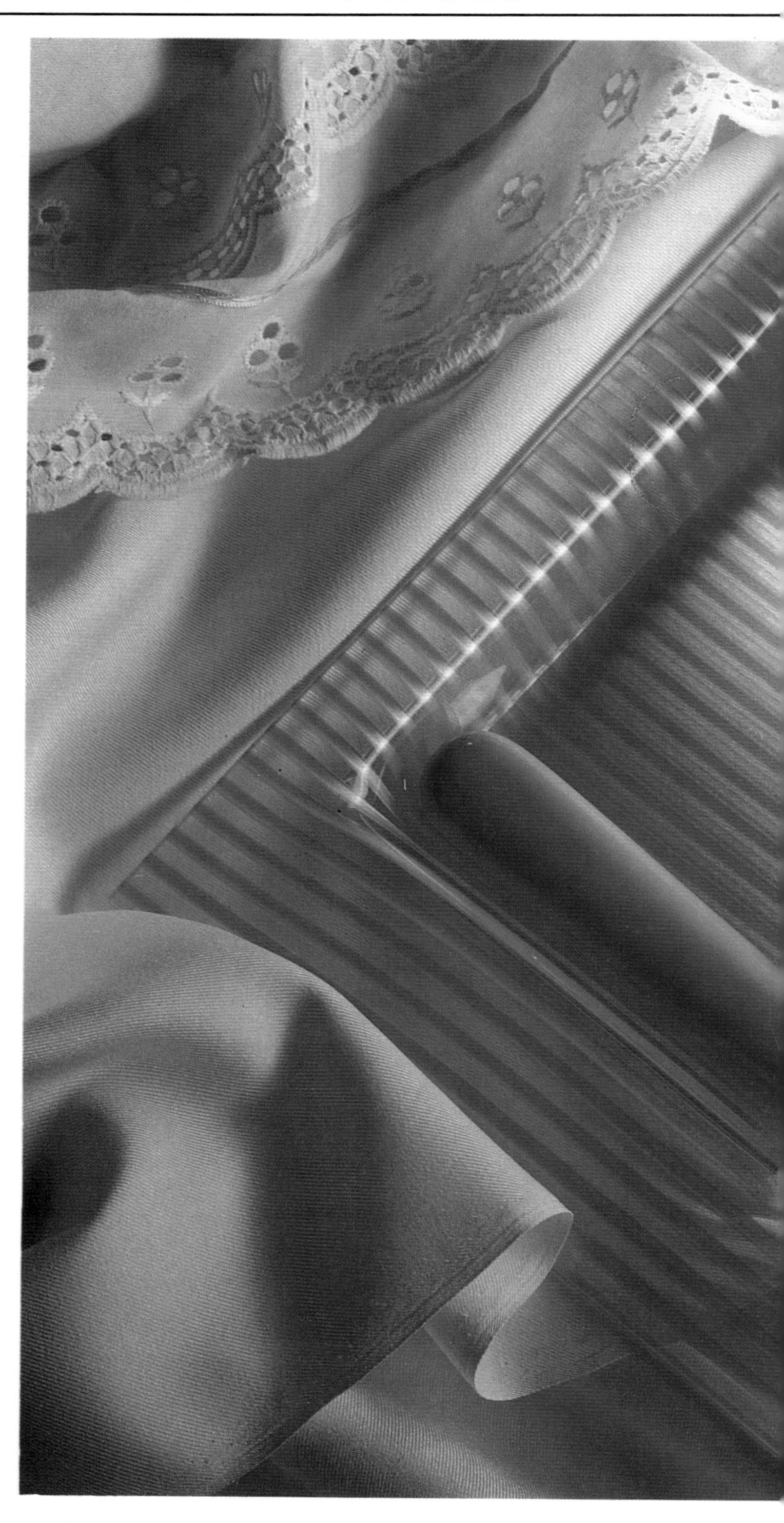

MUSSELS IN WHITE WINE

0.20 | 143 cals

Serves 2

900 g (2 lb) fresh mussels
1 small onion, skinned and finely chopped
1 garlic clove, skinned and crushed
75 ml (5 tbsp) dry white wine
75 ml (5 tbsp) fish stock or water
30 ml (2 tbsp)) chopped fresh parsley
salt and freshly ground pepper

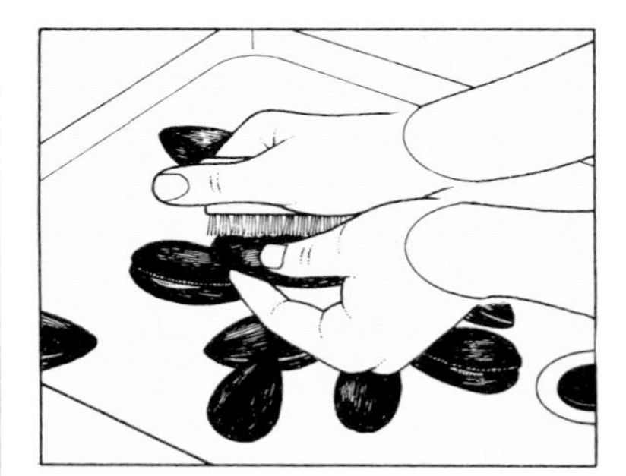

1 To clean the mussels, put them in a sink or bowl and scrub thoroughly with a hard brush. Wash them in several changes of water.

2 Scrape off any 'beards' or tufts protruding from the shells. Discard any damaged mussels or any that do not close when tapped with a knife.

3 Put the onion, garlic, wine, stock and mussels in a large bowl. Cover and cook on HIGH for 3–5 minutes or until all the mussels have opened, removing the mussels on the top as they open and shaking the bowl occasionally. Discard any mussels that have not opened.

4 Pile the mussels in a warmed serving dish. Stir the parsley into the liquid remaining in the bowl and season to taste with salt and pepper. Pour over the mussels and serve immediately with lots of crusty bread.

PRAWNS AND LETTUCE COOKED IN BRANDY AND CREAM

0.15 £ £ 392 cals

Serves 1

175 g (6 oz) medium raw prawns, in the shell

15 g ($\frac{1}{2}$ oz) butter or margarine

salt and freshly ground pepper

25 ml ($1\frac{1}{2}$ tbsp) brandy

45 ml (3 tbsp) double cream

4 green Cos lettuce leaves, shredded

lemon twists, to garnish

Note: if you find it difficult to buy raw prawns, buy the best quality cooked prawns in the shell and omit step 1.

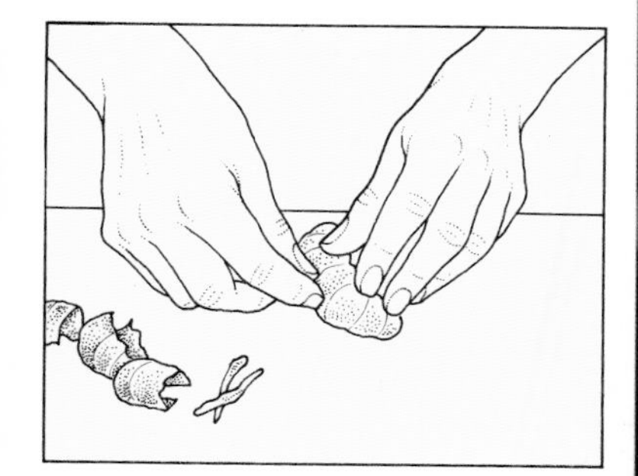

1 Prepare the prawns. Remove the shells, leaving the tail shells intact. Then, with kitchen scissors, split the prawns along the inner curve, stopping at the tail shell, and cutting deep enough to expose the dark vein. Spread each prawn wide open, remove the dark vein then rinse under cold running water. Dry thoroughly on kitchen paper.

2 Put the butter into a medium bowl and cook on HIGH for 45 seconds or until the butter melts. Stir in the prawns and cook on HIGH for $1\frac{1}{2}$–$2\frac{1}{2}$ minutes, or until the prawns just turn pink, stirring frequently. Remove with a slotted spoon and set aside.

3 Season with salt and pepper and quickly stir in the brandy and the cream. Cook on HIGH for 4–$4\frac{1}{2}$ minutes or until the mixture is thickened and reduced.

4 Stir in the prawns and lettuce and mix together carefully. Cook on HIGH for 30–45 seconds or until the prawns are just heated through. Garnish with lemon twists and serve immediately.

Devilled Herrings in Oatmeal

0.10 £ 335 cals

Serves 2

10 ml (2 tsp) tomato purée
2.5 ml ($\frac{1}{2}$ tsp) mild mustard
2.5 ml ($\frac{1}{2}$ tsp) brown sugar
dash of Worcestershire sauce
pinch of cayenne pepper
salt and freshly ground pepper
4 small herring fillets
60 ml (4 tbsp) medium oatmeal
15 ml (1 tbsp) vegetable oil
15 g ($\frac{1}{2}$ oz) butter or margarine
lemon wedges and mustard and cress, to garnish

1 Heat a browning dish on HIGH for 5–8 minutes or according to the manufacturer's instructions.

2 Meanwhile, mix the tomato purée, mustard, sugar, Worcestershire sauce and cayenne pepper together. Season with salt and pepper. Spread the paste thinly on to both sides of each fillet, then coat in the oatmeal.

3 Put the oil and butter or margarine in the browning dish and swirl it around to coat the base of the dish.

4 Quickly add the fillets, skin side down, and cook on HIGH for $1\frac{1}{2}$ minutes. Turn over and cook on HIGH for 1–2 minutes or until the fish is cooked. Serve garnished with lemon wedges and mustard and cress.

Fishcakes

0.30 £ ✳* 223 cals

* before cooking

Makes 4

2 potatoes, each weighing 100 g (4 oz)
225 g (8 oz) fish fillets, such as smoked haddock, cod, salmon or coley
30 ml (2 tbsp) milk
25 g (1 oz) butter or margarine
finely grated rind of $\frac{1}{2}$ lemon
30 ml (2 tbsp) chopped fresh parsley
few drops anchovy essence (optional)
salt and freshly ground pepper
beaten egg
30 ml (2 tbsp) seasoned plain flour
30 ml (2 tbsp) vegetable oil
lime twists, to garnish

1 Scrub the potatoes and prick all over with a fork. Cook on HIGH for 7 minutes, turning over once.

2 Put the fish and the milk in a small shallow dish. Cover and put in the cooker with the potatoes. Cook on HIGH for 4–5 minutes until the fish flakes easily and the potatoes are soft.

3 Cut the potatoes in half, scoop out the flesh and put in a bowl. Flake the fish, discarding the skin, and add to the potato with the cooking liquid.

4 Heat a browning dish on HIGH for 5–8 minutes or according to the manufacturer's instructions.

5 Meanwhile, mix the fish and potato with the butter or margarine, lemon rind, half the parsley, the anchovy essence, if using, and salt and pepper to taste. Mash thoroughly together, then mix with enough beaten egg to bind.

6 Shape into four fishcakes about 2.5 cm (1 inch) thick. Mix the remaining parsley with the seasoned flour and use to coat the fishcakes.

7 Add the oil to the browning dish, then quickly add the fishcakes and cook on HIGH for $2\frac{1}{2}$ minutes. Turn over and cook on HIGH for a further 2 minutes. Serve immediately, garnished with lime twists.

TAGLIATELLE WITH FRESH FIGS

0.10 £ 579 cals

Serves 1

75 g (3 oz) dried tagliatelle
salt and freshly ground pepper
3 large ripe fresh figs
15 g ($\frac{1}{2}$ oz) butter or margarine
1.25 ml ($\frac{1}{4}$ tsp) medium curry powder
30 ml (2 tbsp) soured cream
30 ml (2 tbsp) grated Parmesan cheese
fresh herbs, to garnish (optional)

1 Put the tagliatelle and salt to taste in a medium bowl and pour over 600 ml (1 pint) boiling water. Stir, cover and cook on HIGH for 3–4 minutes or until almost tender, stirring frequently. Leave to stand, covered (do not drain).

2 Meanwhile, cut one of the figs in half lengthways. Reserve one of the halves to garnish, then peel and roughly chop the remainder.

3 Put the butter, chopped figs and curry powder in a shallow dish and cook on HIGH for 2 minutes, stirring occasionally.

4 Drain the pasta and stir into the fig mixture with the soured cream and Parmesan cheese. Season well with salt and pepper. Carefully mix together with two forks and cook on HIGH for 1–2 minutes or until hot.

5 Garnish with fresh herbs, if using, and the reserved fig half and serve immediately.

HOT BAGUETTE SANDWICH WITH SALAMI AND RED PEPPER SAUCE

0.15 £ 920 cals

Serves 2

- 15 ml (1 tbsp) olive or vegetable oil
- 1 small onion, skinned and chopped
- 5 ml (1 tsp) paprika
- 2.5 ml ($\frac{1}{2}$ tsp) sugar
- pinch of cayenne pepper
- 1 small red pepper, cored, seeded and chopped
- 15 ml (1 tbsp) plain flour
- 150 ml ($\frac{1}{4}$ pint) chicken stock
- 1 small baguette, about 30.5 cm (12 inches) long
- 225 g (8 oz) Mozzarella cheese
- 4 thin slices of Danish salami
- freshly ground pepper
- few black olives, stoned (optional)

1 Put the oil, onion, paprika, sugar, cayenne pepper and chopped red pepper in a medium bowl. Cover and cook on HIGH for 5–7 minutes or until softened, stirring occasionally. Stir in the flour and cook on HIGH for 30 seconds.

2 Gradually stir in the chicken stock and cook on HIGH for 5–6 minutes stirring frequently, until the pepper is soft and the sauce has thickened.

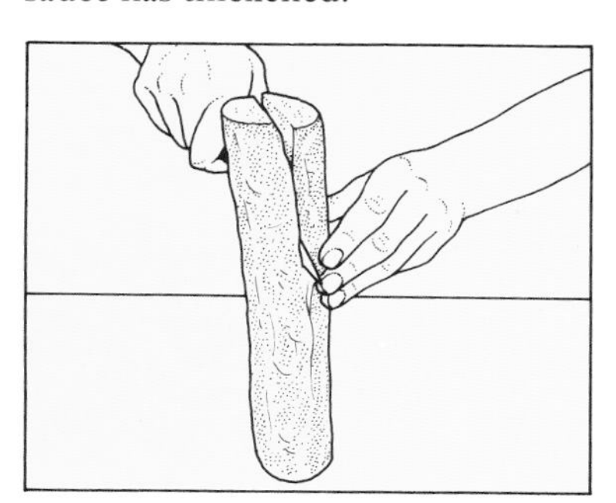

3 Meanwhile, cut the baguette in half widthways, then cut each half in half lengthways. Cut the Mozzarella into thin slices and remove the rind from the salami. Arrange a layer of Mozzarella on two halves. Top with a layer of salami. Season with pepper.

4 When the sauce is cooked, let it cool a little then purée in a blender or food processor until smooth. Spoon on top of the salami. Top with a few olives, if using. Put the other half of the baguette on top of each half to make two sandwiches.

5 Wrap each sandwich in greaseproof paper and cook on HIGH for 1–1$\frac{1}{2}$ minutes or until the sandwiches are just warmed through. Serve immediately.

LAMB BURGERS

0.15 £ ✻* 496 cals

* freeze before step 3

Serves 4

450 g (1 lb) lean minced lamb or beef

1 large onion, skinned and finely grated

5 ml (1 tsp) salt

1.25 ml ($\frac{1}{4}$ tsp) cayenne pepper

30 ml (2 tbsp) vegetable oil

plain or toasted hamburger buns, to serve

tomato ketchup, to serve

1 Mix the lamb and onion together and season to taste with the salt and cayenne pepper.

2 Divide the lamb mixture into four and shape each portion into a neat pattie about 2.5 cm (1 inch) thick.

3 Heat a large browning dish on HIGH for 5–8 minutes or according to manufacturer's instructions.

4 Add the oil, then quickly press two lamb burgers flat on to the hot surface and cook on HIGH for 2–3 minutes. Turn the burgers over, re-position them and cook on HIGH for a further 2–3 minutes or until cooked. Repeat with the remaining burgers.

5 Serve the lamb burgers in plain or toasted hamburger buns, with tomato ketchup.

BEEF WITH GINGER AND GARLIC

0.20* £ £ 510 cals

* plus 1 hour marinating

Serves 2

350 g (12 oz) fillet steak

2.5 cm (1 inch) piece of fresh root ginger, peeled and finely grated

1 garlic clove, skinned and crushed

150 ml ($\frac{1}{4}$ pint) dry sherry

30 ml (2 tbsp) soy sauce

2 medium carrots

15 ml (1 tbsp) vegetable oil

30 ml (2 tbsp) cornflour

2.5 cm ($\frac{1}{2}$ tsp) light soft brown sugar

1 Cut the steak across the grain into 1 cm ($\frac{1}{2}$ inch) strips, and put into a bowl. Mix the ginger with the garlic, sherry and soy sauce, then pour over the steak, making sure that all the meat is coated. Cover and leave to marinate for at least 1 hour. Using a potato peeler, cut the carrots into thin slices lengthways.

2 Put the oil in a large bowl and cook on HIGH for 1 minute or until hot. Using a slotted spoon, remove the steak from the marinade and stir into the hot oil. Cook on HIGH for 1–2 minutes or until the steak is just cooked, stirring once.

3 Meanwhile, blend the cornflour and the sugar with a little of the marinade to make a smooth paste, then gradually blend in all of the marinade.

4 Stir the carrots into the steak and cook on HIGH for 1–2 minutes, then gradually stir in the cornflour and marinade mixture. Cook on HIGH for 2–3 minutes until boiling and thickened, stirring frequently. Serve with rice.

SPICY MINI MEATBALLS WITH TOMATO AND CORIANDER SAUCE

0.25 | 515 cals

Serves 2

1 small onion, skinned and quartered
1 garlic clove, skinned and crushed
2.5 cm (1 inch) piece of fresh root ginger, peeled and crushed
350 g (12 oz) lean minced beef
15 ml (1 tbsp) mango chutney
2.5 ml (½ tsp) ground cumin
2.5 ml (½ tsp) ground coriander
30 ml (2 tbsp) chopped fresh coriander
salt and freshly ground pepper
1 egg, size 6, beaten
200 g (7 oz) can tomatoes
15 ml (1 tbsp) chicken stock
10 ml (2 tsp) tomato purée
5 ml (1 tsp) sugar
fresh coriander, to garnish

1 Put the onion, garlic and ginger in a blender or food processor and liquidise until very finely chopped.

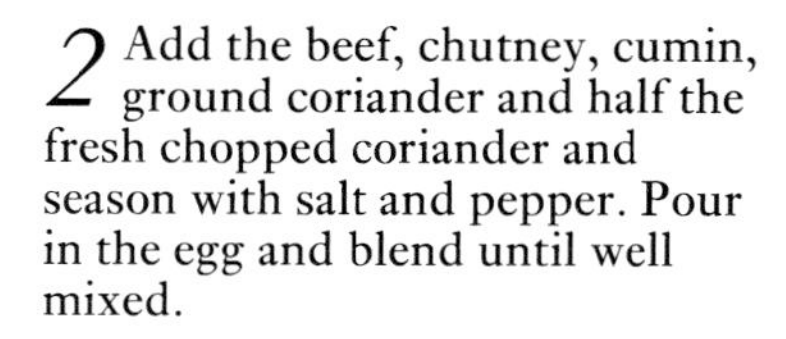

2 Add the beef, chutney, cumin, ground coriander and half the fresh chopped coriander and season with salt and pepper. Pour in the egg and blend until well mixed.

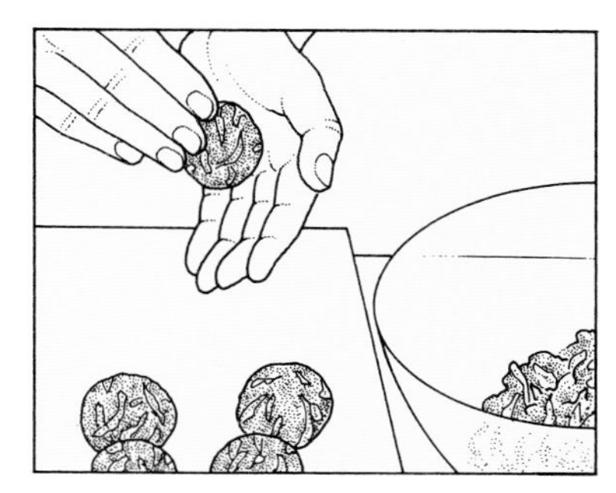

3 Shape the mixture into 16 small balls. Arrange in a single layer in a shallow dish. Cook on HIGH for 5–6 minutes or until the meat is cooked, rearranging once during cooking. Leave to stand, covered, while making the sauce.

4 To make the sauce, put the tomatoes and their juice into a large bowl. Stir in the chicken stock, tomato purée, sugar, salt and pepper.

5 Cook on HIGH for 5 minutes, stirring occasionally, then stir in the remaining fresh coriander and cook on HIGH for 2–3 minutes or until the sauce is reduced and thickened.

6 Cook the meatballs on HIGH for 1–2 minutes or until reheated. Serve the meatballs with the sauce, garnished with coriander.

HONEY ROAST GAMMON

0.30* | 420–560 cals

* plus 10 minutes standing time

Serves 6–8

1.4 kg (3 lb) gammon or collar

30 ml (2 tbsp) clear honey

30 ml (2 tbsp) orange marmalade

few drops of Tabasco sauce

1 Weigh the gammon and calculate the cooking time, allowing 7–8 minutes per 450 g (1 lb). Put the gammon in a roasting bag. Seal the end and prick the bag in several places. Stand on a roasting rack and place in a large shallow dish. Cook on HIGH for the calculated cooking time.

2 Five minutes before the end of the cooking time, remove the rind from the gammon and discard. Mix the honey, marmalade and Tabasco together and brush all over the joint. Continue cooking, uncovered, for the remaining time, brushing frequently with the marinade.

3 Cover tightly with foil and leave to stand for 10 minutes before serving hot or cold.

LAMB WITH AUBERGINE AND MINT

| 1.00 | £ £ ✳ | 338 cals |

Serves 4

- 1 large aubergine, weighing about 400 g (14 oz)
- salt and freshly ground pepper
- 450 g (1 lb) lean boneless lamb, such as fillet or leg
- 30 ml (2 tbsp) olive oil
- 397 g (14 oz) can tomatoes, drained
- a few allspice berries, crushed
- small bunch of fresh mint

1 Cut the aubergine into 2.5 cm (1 inch) cubes. Put in a colander, sprinkling each layer generously with salt. Stand the colander on a large plate, cover with a small plate and place a weight on top. Leave for about 20 minutes to extract the bitter juices.

2 Meanwhile, trim the meat of all excess fat and cut into 2.5 cm (1 inch) cubes. Rinse the aubergine and pat dry.

3 Heat a large browning dish on HIGH for 5–8 minutes or according to manufacturer's instructions.

4 Put the oil in the browning dish, then quickly add the meat. Cook on HIGH for 2 minutes.

5 Turn the pieces of meat over and cook on HIGH for a further 2 minutes. Add the aubergine to the browning dish and cook on HIGH for 5 minutes, stirring once.

6 Add the tomatoes, breaking them up with a fork, the allspice and pepper to taste. Cover and cook on HIGH for about 15 minutes or until the lamb and aubergine are very tender, stirring occasionally.

7 Coarsely chop the mint and stir into the lamb with salt to taste. Re-cover and cook on HIGH for 1 minute.

CALF'S LIVER WITH APPLE, BACON AND SAGE

0.25 £ £ 572 cals

Serves 2

225 g (8 oz) calf's liver, sliced
15 ml (1 tbsp) plain flour
salt and freshly ground pepper
paprika
15 ml (1 tbsp) vegetable oil
15 g ($\frac{1}{2}$ oz) butter or margarine
3 rashers streaky bacon, rinded
1 red eating apple
1 medium onion, skinned and thinly sliced
200 ml (7 fl oz) medium dry cider
30 ml (2 tbsp) soured cream
5 ml (1 tsp) chopped fresh sage or 2.5 ml ($\frac{1}{2}$ tsp) dried
fresh sage, to garnish

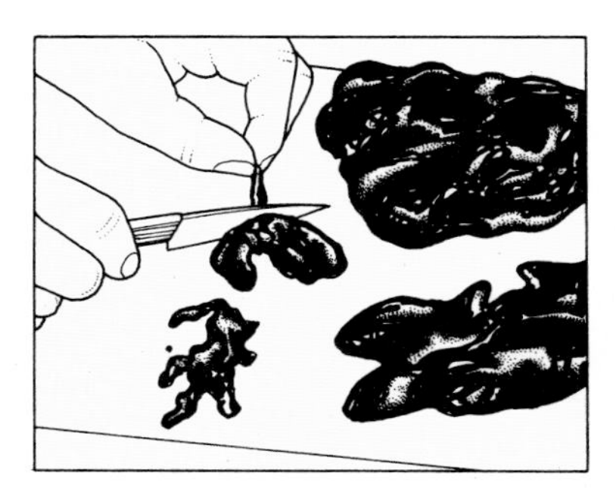

1 Cut the liver into thin strips, trimming away all ducts and gristle. Coat in the flour and season well with salt, pepper and paprika.

2 Cut the bacon into thin strips. Core the apple, cut into rings, then cut each ring in half.

3 Put the oil and the butter into a shallow dish and cook on HIGH for 30 seconds or until the butter melts.

4 Stir the onion and bacon into the fat and cook on HIGH for 5–6 minutes, or until the onion is softened, stirring frequently. Stir in the liver and cook on HIGH for 1–2 minutes or until the liver just changes colour, stirring occasionally. Stir in the apple slices and the cider and cook on HIGH for 2–3 minutes or until the liver is tender, stirring occasionally.

5 Remove the liver, bacon, apple and onion with a slotted spoon and transfer to a warmed serving dish.

6 Stir in the remaining cider, the cream and the sage and cook on HIGH for 4–5 minutes or until thickened and reduced. Adjust the seasoning, if necessary.

7 Cook the liver and apple mixture on HIGH for 1 minute to reheat, if necessary, then pour over the sauce. Garnish with sage and serve immediately.

KIDNEY AND BACON KEBABS

| 0.30 | £ | 344 cals |

Serves 4

700 g ($1\frac{1}{2}$ lb) lamb's kidneys
8 streaky bacon rashers, rinded
100 g (4 oz) button mushrooms
vegetable oil
45 ml (3 tbsp) dry sherry
salt and freshly ground pepper

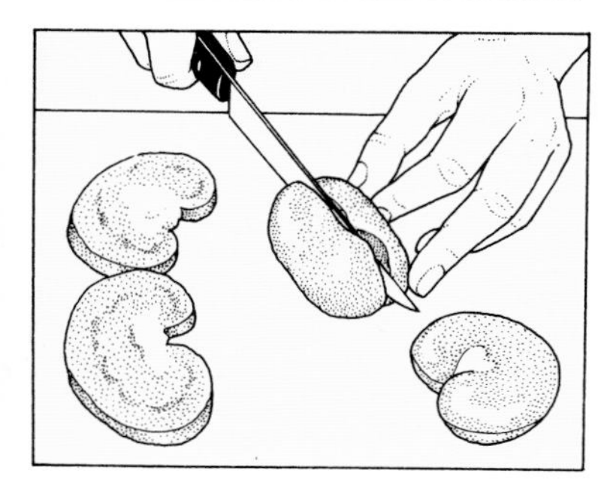

1 Remove the outer membranes from the kidneys and discard. Split each kidney in half lengthways and, using scissors, remove and discard the core. Prick each kidney twice with a fork to prevent them popping during cooking.

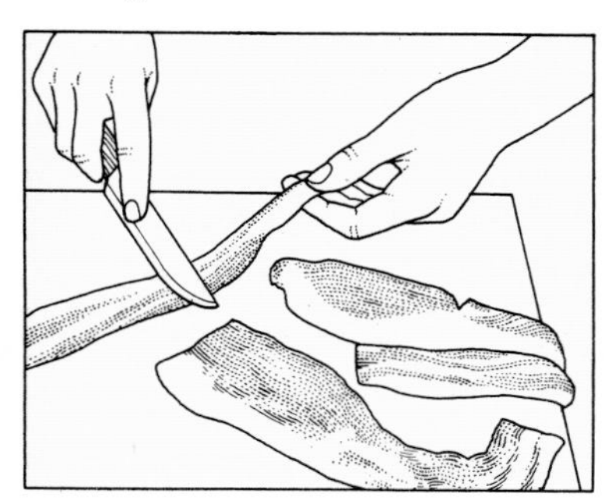

2 Stretch the bacon rashers, using the back of a knife and cut each in half widthways. Roll up to make 16 bacon rolls.

3 Thread the kidneys, bacon rolls and mushrooms on to eight wooden skewers. Arrange on a roasting rack in a single layer, then stand the rack in a large shallow dish. Brush with a little vegetable oil. Cook on HIGH for 8–9 minutes, rearranging and turning once.

4 Remove the kebabs from the cooker and transfer to a serving dish. Add the sherry to the juices collected in the dish and cook on HIGH for 3–4 minutes until boiling and slightly reduced. Season to taste with salt and pepper, then strain over the kebabs. Serve immediately.

PORK AND VEGETABLES

0.10* £ 483 cals

* plus 30 minutes marinating

Serves 4

30 ml (2 tbsp) vegetable oil

60 ml (4 tbsp) soy sauce

15 ml (1 tbsp) dry sherry

12.5 ml ($2\frac{1}{2}$ tsp) cornflour

6.25 ml ($1\frac{1}{4}$ tsp) sugar

2.5 ml ($\frac{1}{2}$ tsp) finely chopped fresh ginger or 1.25 ml ($\frac{1}{4}$ tsp) ground ginger

1 garlic clove, skinned and crushed

450 g (1 lb) pork fillet, cut into thin strips

2 large carrots, peeled and cut into thin strips

1 green pepper, cut into thin strips

3 spring onions, cut into 2.5 cm (1 inch) lengths

225 g (8 oz) mushrooms, sliced

cooked rice, to serve

1 Stir the oil, soy sauce, sherry, cornflour, sugar, ginger and garlic together in a large bowl. Add the pork, mix well and leave to marinate for at least 30 minutes.

2 Stir in the remaining ingredients and cook on HIGH for 7–8 minutes until the pork is tender and the juices run clear and the vegetables are tender but still firm, stirring occasionally. Serve with cooked rice.

SAGE AND BACON-STUFFED PORK

0.40* £ 698–930 cals

* plus 10 minutes standing time

Serves 6–8

about 1.8 kg (4 lb) boned loin of pork

8 streaky bacon rashers, rinded

12 fresh sage leaves

2 garlic cloves, skinned and cut into slivers

salt and freshly ground pepper

fresh sage, to garnish

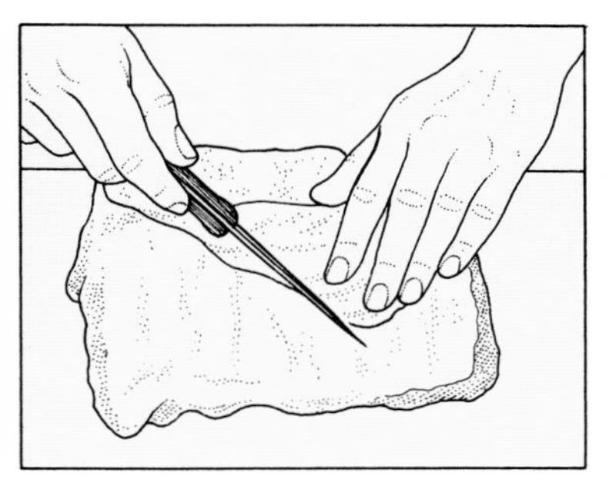

1 Cut the rind off the pork, together with all but a very thin layer of fat next to the meat. Score the remaining fat with a sharp knife.

2 Turn over the meat and lay half of the bacon, the sage leaves and the garlic over the flesh. Season well with salt and pepper. Roll up and lay the remaining bacon on top.

3 Secure the joint with fine string. Weigh the joint and calculate the cooking time allowing 8 minutes per 450 g (1 lb). Place on a roasting rack, bacon side down, and cover with a split roasting bag. Stand the rack in a shallow dish to catch the juices. Cook on HIGH for half of the calculated cooking time, then turn over and cook for the remaining time.

4 Wrap tightly in foil and leave to stand for 10 minutes. Serve cut into slices, garnished with fresh sage leaves.

GRAVY

Gravy to serve with the joint is best made conventionally while the meat is standing. Transfer 30 ml (2 tbsp) fat (collected in the dish after cooking) to a saucepan, then stir in 20 ml (4 tsp) flour. Cook for 2–3 minutes until brown, stirring all the time, then pour in 450 ml ($\frac{3}{4}$ pint) beef stock and season to taste with salt and pepper. Bring to the boil and simmer gently.

ROAST CHICKEN

0.45* | 400 cals

* plus 10–15 minutes standing time

Serves 4

1.8 kg (4 lb) oven-ready roasting chicken

salt and freshly ground pepper

few fresh herbs (optional)

stuffing (optional)

1 Season the inside of the chicken with salt and pepper. Place herbs inside the chicken and stuff the neck end if wished.

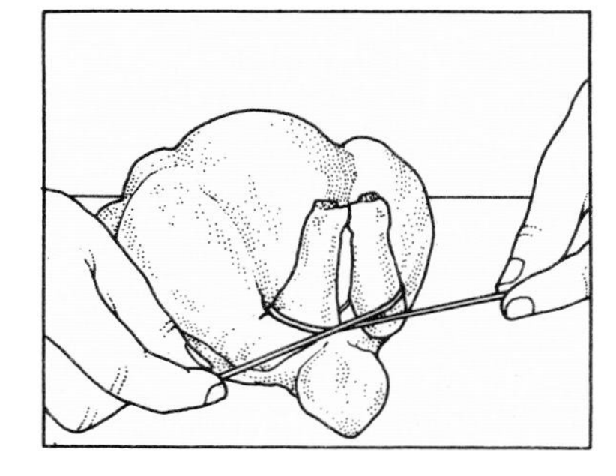

2 Truss the chicken into a neat compact shape using fine string. Weigh the bird and calculate the cooking time allowing 8–10 minutes per 450 g (1 lb).

3 Stand the bird on a roasting rack, breast side down, and stand the rack in a shallow dish to catch the juices. Cover with a split roasting bag and cook for half of the calculated time. Turn over, re-cover and continue to cook for the remaining time.

4 Cover tightly with foil and leave to stand for 10–15 minutes before serving. Brown and crisp under a hot grill, if liked.

ROAST CHICKEN

Because it cooks so quickly and the method of cooking uses moist rather than dry heat, the skin of roast chicken will not be very brown, nor will it be crisp. To help it brown a little and to reduce splattering, cover with a split roasting bag. Commercially prepared browning agents are available, or paprika, honey, soy sauce or Worcestershire sauce may be brushed or sprinkled on to the skin before cooking. To achieve a brown and crisp skin, simply cook under a hot grill for a few minutes.

MARINATED CHICKEN WITH PEPPERS AND MARJORAM

0.15* £ 655 cals

* plus 30 minutes marinating

Serves 2

2 chicken breast fillets, skinned

1 garlic clove, skinned and crushed

10 ml (2 tsp) lemon juice

pinch of sugar

45 ml (3 tbsp) olive or vegetable oil

15 ml (1 tbsp) chopped fresh marjoram or 5 ml (1 tsp) dried

1 small onion, skinned and thinly sliced into rings

salt and freshly ground pepper

1 small red pepper, cored, seeded and coarsely chopped

1 small yellow pepper, cored, seeded and coarsely chopped

50 g (2 oz) black olives, halved and stoned

15 ml (1 tbsp) capers

fresh marjoram, to garnish

1 Cut the chicken breasts in half widthways, and put into a shallow dish just large enough to hold them in a single layer.

2 Put the garlic, lemon juice and sugar in a small bowl and whisk together. Gradually whisk in the oil. Stir in the marjoram, onion rings, salt and pepper.

3 Pour over the chicken, cover and leave to marinate for at least 30 minutes.

4 Meanwhile, put the peppers into a shallow dish with 30 ml (2 tbsp) water, cover and cook on HIGH for 5–6 minutes or until the peppers are just soft, stirring occasionally. Drain and set aside.

5 To cook the chicken, cover and cook on HIGH for 5–6 minutes or until the chicken is tender, turning once.

6 Add the peppers, olives and capers and cook on HIGH for 1–2 minutes or until heated through, stirring once. Serve immediately, garnished with fresh marjoram.

SOLE AND SPINACH ROULADES

0.15 £ £ 255 cals

Serves 4

12 sole fillets, each weighing about 75 g (3 oz), skinned
5 ml (1 tsp) fennel seeds, crushed
salt and freshly ground pepper
12 spinach or sorrel leaves, washed
15 ml (1 tbsp) dry white wine
45 ml (3 tbsp) Greek strained yogurt
pinch of ground turmeric
spinach or sorrel leaves, to garnish

1 Place the sole fillets, skinned side up, on a chopping board. Sprinkle with the fennel seeds and season to taste with salt and pepper. Lay a spinach or sorrel leaf, vein side up on top of each fillet, then roll up and secure with a wooden cocktail stick.

2 Arrange the fish in a circle around the edge of a large shallow dish and pour over the wine. Cover and cook on HIGH for 6–7 minutes until tender. Using a slotted spoon, transfer the fish to a serving plate.

3 Gradually stir the yogurt and turmeric into the cooking liquid. Season to taste with salt and pepper and cook on HIGH for 1–2 minutes until slightly thickened, stirring occasionally. Serve the roulades with a little of the sauce poured over, garnished with spinach or sorrel leaves.

Haddock Mousse

0.25* ⊟ £ 940 cals

* plus 2 hours setting

Serves 4

450 g (1 lb) haddock fillet
15 ml (1 tbsp) gelatine
50 ml (2 fl oz) white wine vinegar
4 hard-boiled eggs, shelled
450 ml ($\frac{3}{4}$ pint) mayonnaise
10 ml (2 tsp) tomato purée
5 ml (1 tsp) anchovy essence
salt and freshly ground pepper
2 egg whites
1 small bunch watercress, trimmed and finely chopped
dill sprig, to garnish

1 Arrange the fish in a single layer in a shallow dish. Cover and cook on HIGH for 6 minutes or until tender. Flake the fish, discarding skin and bones.

2 Sprinkle the gelatine over the vinegar in a small bowl. Leave to soften slightly then add 225 ml (8 fl oz) hot water. Cook on HIGH for 30 seconds or until the gelatine is dissolved.

3 Place the hard-boiled eggs, 150 ml ($\frac{1}{4}$ pint) mayonnaise, tomato purée, anchovy essence, salt and pepper and fish in a blender or food processor and liquidise until smooth. Gradually stir in the gelatine. Tip into a bowl and refrigerate just until the mixture is thick enough to coat the back of a spoon.

4 Whisk the egg whites until stiff and fold into the fish mixture. Spoon into a 1.7–2.3 litre (3–4 pint) ring mould and refrigerate for about 2 hours until set.

5 Beat the finely chopped watercress into the remaining mayonnaise and set aside.

6 To serve, quickly dip the mould into hot water to loosen the mousse, then turn out on to a serving plate. Spoon over a little of the green mayonnaise and garnish with the dill sprig. Serve the remaining mayonnaise separately.

Monkfish in White Wine

0.30 £ £ 286 cals

Serves 4

25 g (1 oz) butter or margarine
1 large onion, skinned and chopped
1 garlic clove, skinned and crushed
450 g (1 lb) courgettes, trimmed and sliced
30 ml (2 tbsp) plain flour
15 ml (1 tbsp) paprika
150 ml ($\frac{1}{4}$ pint) dry white wine
150 ml ($\frac{1}{4}$ pint) fish or chicken stock
225 g (8 oz) tomatoes, skinned, seeded and chopped
15 ml (1 tbsp) fresh basil or 5 ml (1 tsp) dried
salt and freshly ground pepper
900 g (2 lb) monkfish, skinned, boned and cut into 5 cm (2 inch) pieces

1 Put the butter in a large bowl and cook on HIGH for 45 seconds or until the butter melts. Add the onion and garlic and cook on HIGH for 5–7 minutes or until the onion is softened, stirring once. Add the courgettes, cover and cook on HIGH for 2 minutes.

2 Stir in the flour, paprika, wine, stock, tomatoes, basil and salt and pepper. Cook on HIGH for 5 minutes or until the liquid is boiling, then continue to cook on HIGH for a further 5 minutes.

3 Add the fish, cover and cook on HIGH for 10 minutes or until the fish is tender, stirring once.

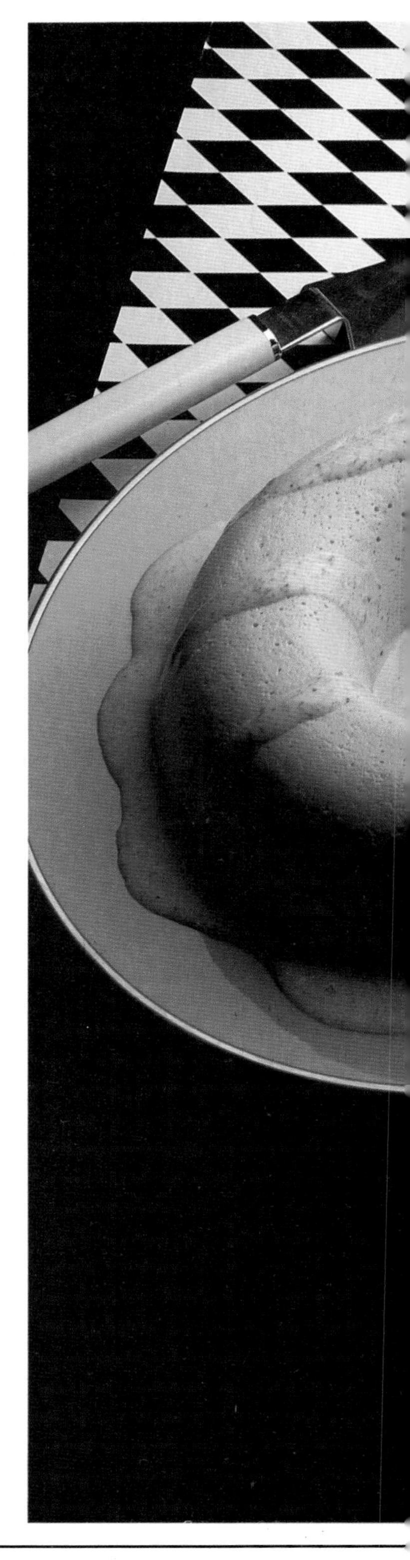

MIXED SEAFOOD WITH SAFFRON SAUCE

0.20 £ £ 167 cals

Serves 4

large pinch of saffron
50 ml (2 fl oz) dry white wine
strip of orange rind
1 bay leaf
4 plaice quarter-cut fillets, each weighing about 50 g (2 oz)
450 g (1 lb) cod fillet
4 cooked unpeeled jumbo prawns (optional)
15 ml (1 tbsp) Greek strained yogurt
salt and freshly ground pepper
fresh herbs, to garnish

1 Put the saffron, wine, orange rind and bay leaf in a small bowl. Cook on HIGH for 2–3 minutes or until boiling. Set aside to infuse while cooking the fish.

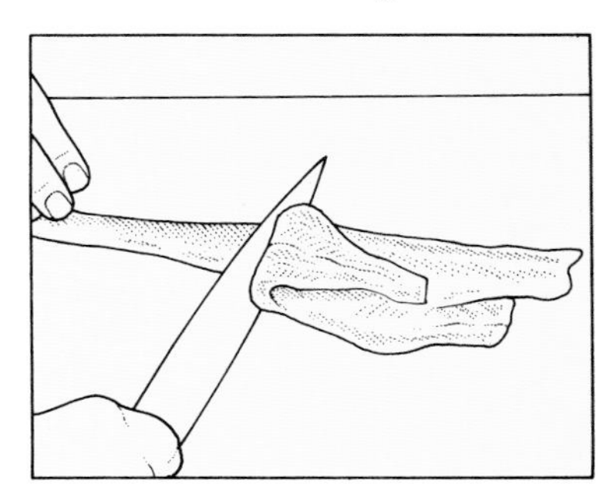

2 Skin the plaice fillets. Lay them flat, skin side down, on a board or work surface. Dip your fingers in salt and grip the tail end, then separate the flesh from the skin at this point with a sharp knife. Work the knife slowly between the skin and flesh using a sawing action until the opposite end of the fillet is reached. Cut each fillet in half widthways. Skin and cut the cod fillets into large chunks.

3 Arrange the fish and prawns, if using, in a single layer in a large shallow dish, placing the thinner pieces and the prawns towards the centre.

4 Pour over 30 ml (2 tbsp) of the infused sauce. Cover and cook on HIGH for 5–6 minutes or until the fish is tender. Transfer the fish to four warmed serving plates.

5 Strain the remaining wine mixture into the cooking juices remaining in the dish and stir in the yogurt. Season to taste with salt and pepper. Cook on HIGH for 1–2 minutes or until hot. Pour over the fish, garnish with herbs and serve immediately.

FRESH PASTA WITH COURGETTES AND SMOKED TROUT

0.20 £ £ 566 cals

Serves 2

2 medium courgettes
15 ml (1 tbsp) olive oil
pinch of saffron
225 g (8 oz) fresh spinach pasta, such as tagliatelle
salt and freshly ground pepper
1 smoked trout, weighing about 225 g (8 oz)
150 ml (¼ pint) crème fraîche or double cream
30 ml (2 tbsp) black lumpfish roe
fresh herb sprigs, to garnish

1 Cut the courgettes into very thin diagonal slices. Cut each slice in half. Put the courgettes, oil and saffron in a medium bowl and cook on HIGH for 1 minute, stirring once.

2 Put the spinach pasta and salt to taste in a large bowl. Pour over enough boiling water to cover by about 2.5 cm (1 inch). Cover and cook on HIGH for 3–4 minutes or until almost tender. Leave to stand, covered, while finishing the sauce. Do not drain.

3 To finish the sauce, flake the trout flesh, discarding the skin and bones. Stir into the courgettes with the crème fraîche or cream and salt and pepper to taste. Cook on HIGH for 2 minutes until hot and slightly thickened.

4 Drain the pasta and return to the large bowl. Pour over the sauce and toss together to mix. If necessary, reheat the sauce and pasta together on HIGH for about 2 minutes. Transfer the pasta to four plates, top each with a spoonful of lumpfish roe and garnish with a herb sprig.

BEAN GOULASH

0.40	164–242 cals

Serves 4–6

100 g (4 oz) black-eye beans, soaked overnight
100 g (4 oz) aduki beans, soaked overnight
15 ml (1 tbsp) vegetable oil
1 garlic clove, skinned and crushed
1 yellow pepper, seeded and roughly chopped
10 ml (2 tsp) caraway seeds, lightly crushed
15 ml (1 tbsp) paprika
397 g (14 oz) can chopped tomatoes
175 g (6 oz) mushrooms, thickly sliced
60 ml (4 tbsp) natural yogurt
salt and freshly ground pepper
chopped fresh parsley, to garnish

1 Drain the beans, rinse well under cold running water and put in a large bowl. Pour over enough boiling water to cover by about 2.5 cm (1 inch). Cover and cook on HIGH for 25–30 minutes or until tender. Leave to stand, covered. Do not drain.

2 Meanwhile, put the oil, garlic, yellow pepper, caraway seeds and paprika in a large serving bowl. Cover and cook on HIGH for 2 minutes, stirring once.

3 Drain the beans, rinse with boiling water and add to the pepper with the tomatoes and mushrooms. Re-cover and cook on HIGH for 8–10 minutes, stirring once.

4 Stir in 30 ml (2 tbsp) of the yogurt and season to taste with salt and pepper. Drizzle the remaining yogurt on top and sprinkle with the parsley. Serve hot with brown rice.

CUCUMBER WITH ONION AND TARRAGON

0.30 | 40 cals

Serves 4

1 cucumber
salt and freshly ground pepper
15 g (½ oz) butter or margarine
30 ml (2 tbsp) chopped fresh tarragon
1 bunch of spring onions, trimmed and sliced
fresh tarragon sprigs, to garnish

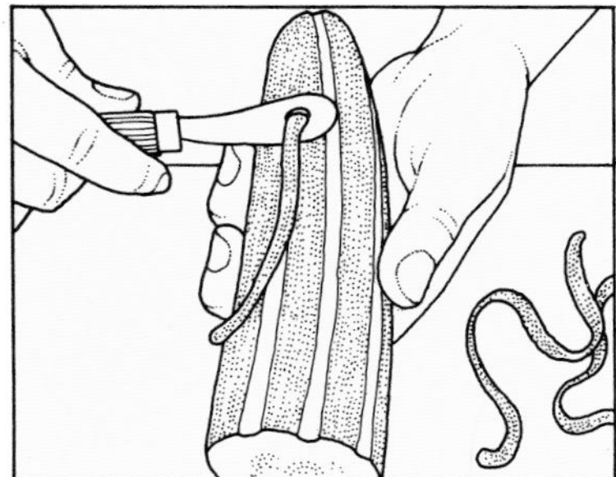

1 Remove thin strips of skin evenly from all round the cucumber. Quarter the cucumber lengthways and cut into 5 cm (2 inch) chunks. Sprinkle with salt. Leave for 20 minutes, then drain and pat dry.

2 Put the cucumber, butter, tarragon and pepper to taste into a large bowl and cover. Cook on HIGH for 1 minute, then add the spring onions and cook on HIGH for 2 minutes or until tender. Season with pepper, then serve garnished with tarragon.

GLAZED VEGETABLES PROVENÇAL

0.20 | £ | 90 cals

Serves 4

30 ml (2 tbsp) vegetable oil
1 garlic clove, skinned and crushed
½ red pepper
½ yellow pepper
½ green pepper
1 courgette, trimmed
1 large tomato
50 g (2 oz) mange-tout, trimmed
60 ml (4 tbsp) dry white wine
salt and freshly ground pepper
fresh basil, to garnish

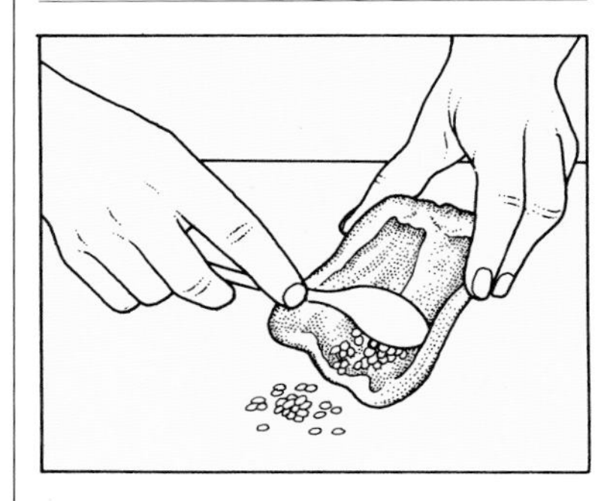

1 Remove the core and seeds from the peppers then cut the flesh into thin strips. Thinly slice the courgette. Skin, seed and cut the flesh of the tomato into strips.

2 Heat a browning dish on HIGH for 5–8 minutes or according to manufacturer's instructions. Add the oil and garlic for the last 30 seconds.

3 Add the vegetables and stir. Cook on HIGH for 2–3 minutes or until the vegetables are slightly softened.

4 Stir in the white wine and season to taste with salt and pepper. Cook on HIGH for 1 minute. Transfer to a serving dish and garnish with fresh basil.

LENTIL, MINT AND YOGURT SALAD

0.45 | 284 cals

Serves 2

100 g (4 oz) green lentils, washed
bouquet garni
60 ml (4 tbsp) olive or vegetable oil
30 ml (2 tbsp) lemon juice
large pinch of ground allspice
salt and freshly ground pepper
45 ml (3 tbsp) chopped fresh mint
4 spring onions
3 large tomatoes
30 ml (2 tbsp) Greek strained yogurt
lemon wedges and mint sprigs, to garnish

VARIATIONS

Lentil and garlic salad: omit the mint and add 2 garlic cloves, skinned and crushed.
Lentil and fresh herb salad: omit the mint and add 45 ml (3 tbsp) chopped fresh parsley.

1 Put the lentils into a large bowl and pour over 900 ml ($1\frac{1}{2}$ pints) boiling water. Add the bouquet garni, cover and cook on HIGH for 10–12 minutes or until the lentils are just tender.

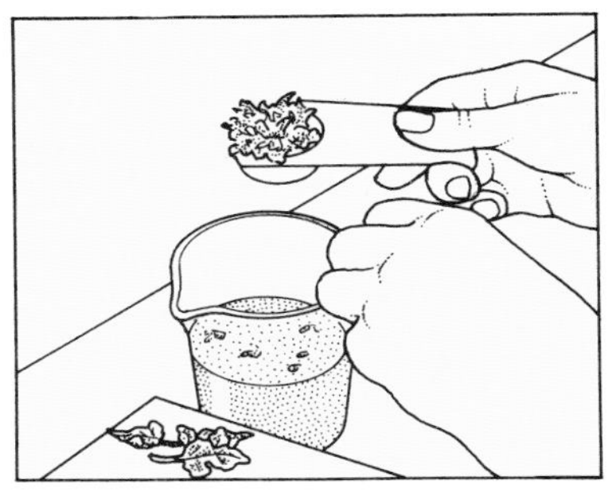

2 Meanwhile, mix together the olive oil and lemon juice and season with allspice, salt and pepper. Stir in the mint.

3 Drain the lentils and stir in the dressing whilst they are still hot so that they absorb the flavour of the dressing. Chill for at least 30 minutes.

4 Meanwhile, trim and chop the spring onions finely and cut the tomatoes into small wedges.

5 Stir into the chilled lentils and mix together well. Stir in the yogurt. Season if necessary. Serve chilled, garnished with lemon wedges and mint sprigs.

LENTIL, MINT AND YOGURT SALAD
Lentils are a useful pulse to keep in the store cupboard because they do not need to be soaked before cooking and you therefore do not have to remember to pre-soak them the night before! Instead of measuring the water for cooking, an alternative method is to pour enough boiling water over the lentils to cover them by about 2.5 cm (1 inch). Always boil the water in a kettle because large quantities are slow to heat up in the microwave cooker.

BABY CARROTS WITH WATERCRESS AND ORANGE

0.15 | 55 cals

Serves 4

bunch of watercress
450 g (1 lb) whole new carrots, scrubbed
15 g ($\frac{1}{2}$ oz) butter or margarine
60 ml (4 tbsp) orange juice
pepper

1 Wash the watercress and reserve a few sprigs for garnish. Cut away any coarse stalks. Chop the leaves and remaining stalks.

2 Put the watercress and carrots in a shallow dish. Dot with the butter and spoon over the orange juice. Season to taste with pepper only.

3 Cover and cook on HIGH for 10–12 minutes or until tender.

OKRA WITH BABY ONIONS AND CORIANDER

0.10 | 43–64 cals

Serves 4–6

450 g (1 lb) okra
15 ml (1 tbsp) olive oil
15 ml (1 tbsp) coriander seeds, crushed
1 garlic clove, skinned and crushed
225 g (8 oz) baby onions, skinned and halved
60 ml (4 tbsp) vegetable stock
salt and freshly ground pepper

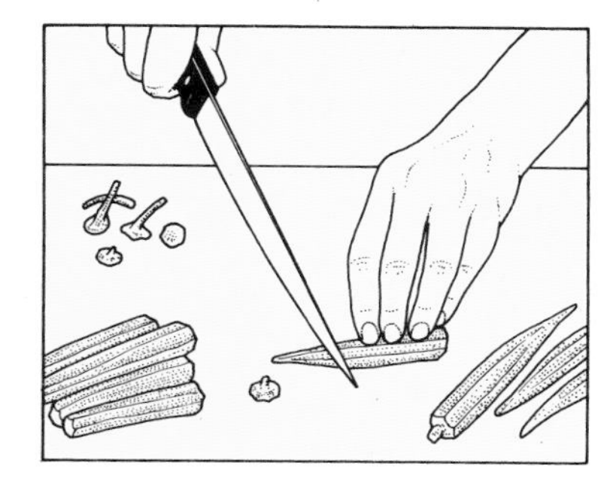

1 Trim off the tops and tails of the okra. Put the oil, coriander and garlic in a serving bowl. Cook on HIGH for 2 minutes.

2 Add the onions, okra and stock and mix well together. Cover and cook on HIGH for 5–7 minutes or until the onions and okra are tender, stirring occasionally. Season to taste with salt and pepper and serve hot.

POTATO AND LEEK RAMEKINS

0.25 | 220 cals

Serves 2

1 large potato, weighing about 225 g (8 oz)

1 small leek

45 ml (3 tbsp) milk

salt and freshly ground pepper

freshly grated nutmeg

1 egg yolk

15 g (½ oz) butter or margarine

5 ml (1 tsp) poppy seeds

1 Grease and line the bases of two 150 ml (¼ pint) ramekin dishes with greaseproof paper.

2 Prick the potato all over with a fork, place on absorbent kitchen paper and cook on HIGH for 5–6 minutes or until soft, turning over halfway through cooking.

3 Meanwhile, finely chop the white part of the leek and slice the green part into very thin 4 cm (1½ inch) long strips. Wash separately and drain well.

4 Put the white leek into a medium bowl with the milk, cover and cook on HIGH for 2–3 minutes or until very soft, stirring occasionally.

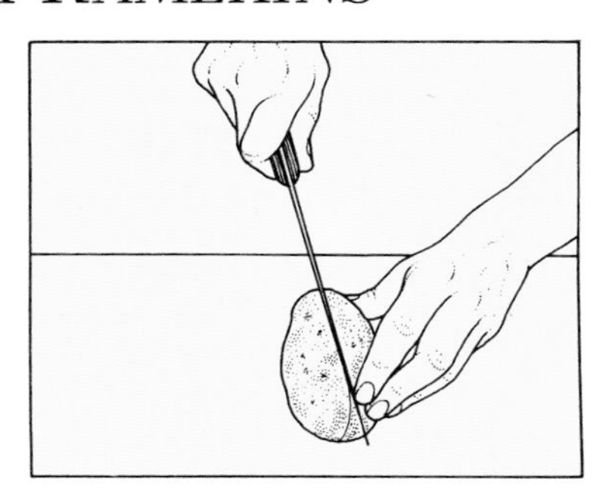

5 Cut the potato in half, scoop out the flesh and stir into the cooked leek and milk. Mash well together and season with salt, pepper and nutmeg. Stir in the egg yolk.

6 Spoon the mixture into the prepared ramekin dishes. Cook on HIGH for 2–2½ minutes or until firm to the touch. Leave to stand.

7 Meanwhile, put the butter into a small bowl with the strips of green leek and the poppy seeds. Cover and cook on HIGH for 2–3 minutes or until tender, stirring occasionally. Season with salt and pepper.

8 Turn the ramekins out on to a serving plate and spoon over the leek mixture. Cook on HIGH for 1–2 minutes to heat through. Serve immediately.

CHERRY TOMATOES WITH PINE NUT AND BASIL DRESSING

0.05 | £ | 170 cals

Serves 2

15 ml (1 tbsp) olive or vegetable oil

25 g (1 oz) pine nuts

2.5 ml (½ tsp) Dijon mustard

2.5 ml (½ tsp) brown sugar

salt and freshly ground pepper

2.5 ml (½ tsp) white wine vinegar

225 g (8 oz) cherry tomatoes, cut in halves

15 ml (1 tbsp) chopped fresh basil

1 Put the oil and the nuts in a medium bowl and cook on HIGH for 2–3 minutes, stirring frequently.

2 Stir in the mustard, sugar, salt and pepper and whisk together with a fork. Whisk in the vinegar.

3 Add the tomatoes and cook on HIGH for 30 seconds, or until the tomatoes are just warm. Stir in the basil and serve immediately.

Apple and Blackcurrant Crumble

0.20 £ ✱ 552–736 cals

Serves 3–4

75 g (3 oz) butter or margarine
75 g (3 oz) plain wholemeal flour
25 g (1 oz) rolled oats
25 g (1 oz) sunflower seeds (optional)
15 g ($\frac{1}{2}$ oz) desiccated coconut
25 g (1 oz) chopped mixed nuts (optional)
25 g (1 oz) light soft brown sugar
5 ml (1 tsp) ground cinnamon (optional)
2.5 ml ($\frac{1}{2}$ tsp) ground mixed spice (optional)
225 g (8 oz) eating apples
225 g (8 oz) blackcurrants
custard, to serve (see below)

1 Put the butter or margarine and flour into a bowl and rub in until the mixture resembles fine breadcrumbs. Stir in the dry ingredients and mix thoroughly together.

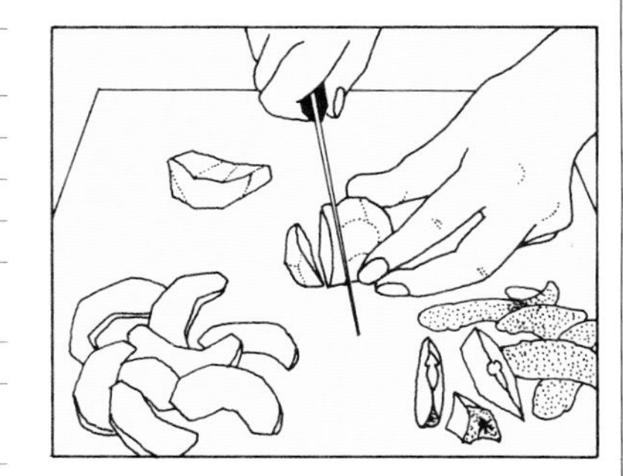

2 Peel, quarter, core and slice the apples. Put in a 1.1 litre (2 pint) deep ovenproof dish with the blackcurrants. Spoon the crumble mixture evenly over the fruit and press down lightly. Cook on HIGH for 11–12 minutes or until the fruit is tender. Serve hot or cold with yogurt, cream or custard.

Blackcurrant Jelly with Fresh Fruit

0.10* £ 83 cals

* plus 3–4 hours chilling

Serves 4

225 g (8 oz) blackcurrants, stringed
finely grated rind and juice of $\frac{1}{2}$ lemon
15 ml (1 tbsp) gelatine
300 ml ($\frac{1}{2}$ pint) unsweetened apple juice
prepared fruit in season, to serve
few mint sprigs, to decorate

1 Put the blackcurrants and lemon rind and juice in a medium bowl. Cook on HIGH for 5–6 minutes or until the blackcurrants are soft, stirring occasionally.

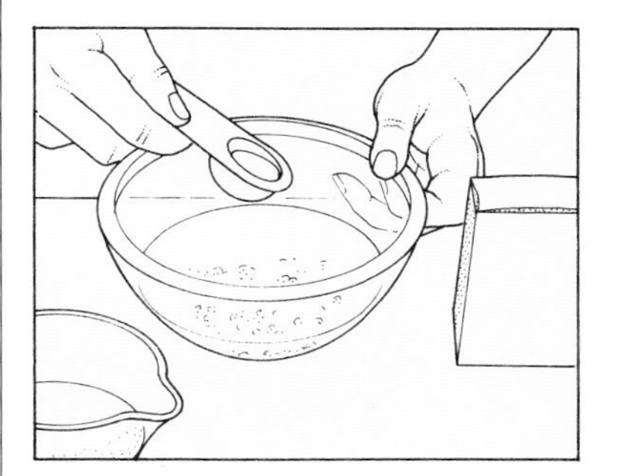

2 Put the gelatine and half of the apple juice in a small bowl and leave to soak for 1 minute. Cook on HIGH for 30–50 seconds until the gelatine is dissolved, stirring frequently. Stir into the blackcurrant mixture with the remaining apple juice.

3 Pour the jelly into four 150 ml ($\frac{1}{4}$ pint) wetted moulds or ramekins and chill for 3–4 hours until set.

4 When set, turn out on to individual plates and arrange the prepared fruit attractively around the jellies. Decorate with mint sprigs, if wished.

FRESH FRUIT TARTLETS

0.45* £ £ 460 cals

* plus 50 minutes chilling and cooling

Makes 8

200 g (7 oz) plain white flour

25 g (1 oz) plain wholemeal flour

75 g (3 oz) caster sugar

25 g (1 oz) hazelnuts, toasted and ground

pinch of salt

50 g (2 oz) butter or margarine

3 eggs, beaten

25 g (1 oz) cornflour

300 ml ($\frac{1}{2}$ pint) milk

few drops of vanilla flavouring

300 ml ($\frac{1}{2}$ pint) double cream

prepared fresh fruit, such as figs, strawberries, raspberries, cherries, kiwi fruit, grapes

30 ml (2 tbsp) apricot conserve

5 ml (1 tsp) lemon juice

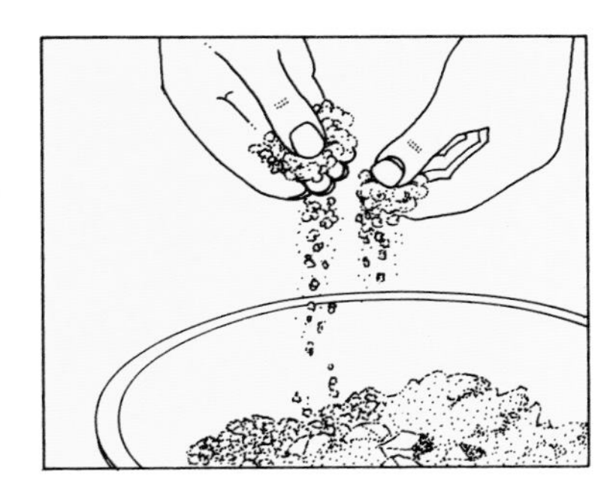

1 Mix 175 g (6 oz) of the plain flour, the wholemeal flour, 25 g (1 oz) of the sugar, the hazelnuts and salt in a bowl. Rub in the fat until the mixture resembles fine breadcrumbs. Add the egg and enough water to make a dough.

2 Turn on to a lightly floured surface and knead for a few seconds until smooth. Wrap in greaseproof paper and chill for 20–30 minutes until firm.

3 Cut the pastry in half, then roll out one half very thinly on a lightly floured surface. Use to cover the base and sides of four inverted 10 cm (4 inch) shallow glass flan dishes.

4 Prick all over with a fork and cook on HIGH, pastry side uppermost for $2\frac{1}{2}$–3 minutes or until the pastry is firm to the touch. Remove the pastry cases from the dishes and invert on to a wire rack to cool. Repeat with the remaining pastry to make eight pastry cases.

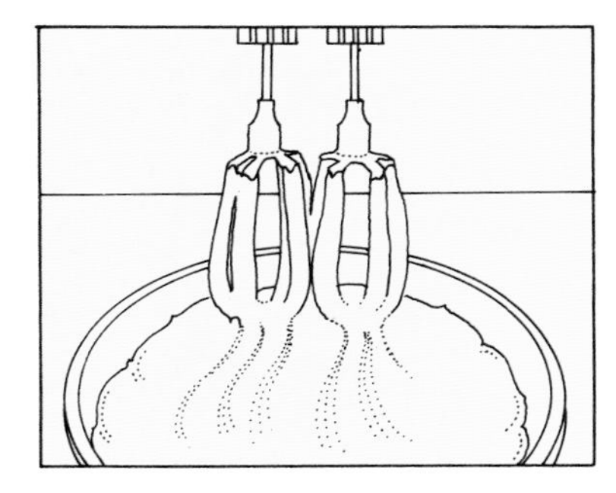

5 To make the filling, put the remaining eggs and sugar in a large bowl and whisk until pale and creamy and the mixture leaves a trail when the whisk is lifted. Sift in the remaining flour and the cornflour, then beat well.

6 Put the milk in a bowl and cook on HIGH for 2–$2\frac{1}{2}$ minutes until just boiling. Gradually pour on the egg mixture, stirring all the time. Add the vanilla flavouring.

7 Cook on HIGH for $1\frac{1}{2}$–2 minutes until very thick, stirring frequently. Cover and leave to cool.

8 When cold, whip the cream until it just holds its shape, then fold into the custard. Fill the pastry cases with the mixture and decorate with fruit.

9 Put the apricot conserve and lemon juice in a small bowl and cook on HIGH for 30 seconds until melted. Carefully brush over the fruit to glaze. Serve as soon as possible.

ALMOND-STUFFED PEACHES

0.10* | 110 cals

* plus 5 minutes standing time

Serves 4

4 firm ripe peaches

50 g (2 oz) ground almonds

finely grated rind of ½ orange

5 ml (1 tsp) clear honey

150 ml (¼ pint) unsweetened orange juice

15 ml (1 tbsp) Amaretto (optional)

a few mint leaves, to decorate

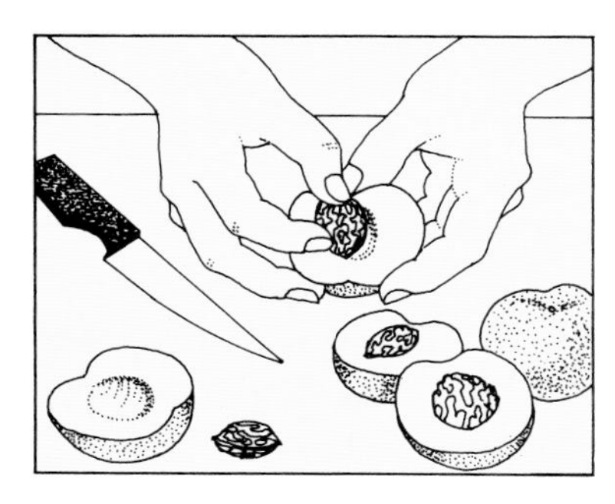

1 Cut the peaches in half and carefully ease out the stones with finger and thumb.

2 Make the hollows in the peaches a little deeper with a teaspoon and reserve the removed flesh.

3 Finely chop the removed peach flesh and mix with the almonds, orange rind, honey and 15 ml (1 tbsp) of the orange juice.

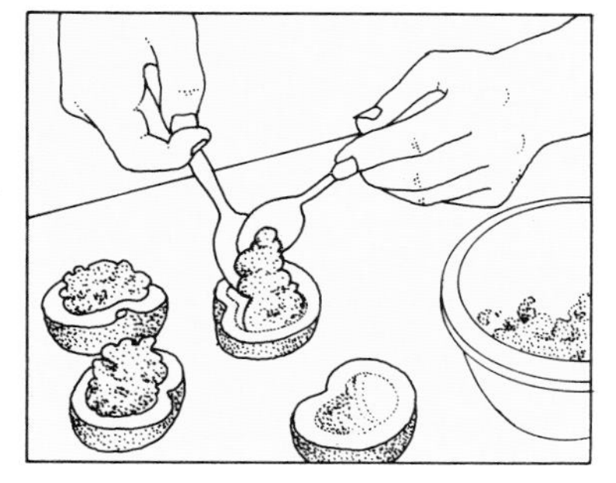

4 Use this mixture to stuff the hollows of the peach halves, mounding the filling slightly.

5 Place the peaches around the edge of a large shallow dish. Mix the remaining orange juice with the Amaretto, if using, and pour around the peaches.

6 Cover and cook on HIGH for 3–5 minutes or until the peaches are tender. Leave to stand for 5 minutes, then serve warm with the juices spooned over and decorated with mint.

SUMMER PUDDINGS

0.15* ⊟ £ ✳ 128 cals

* plus overnight chilling

Serves 2

5–6 thin slices of day old white bread

150 g (5 oz) strawberries

150 g (5 oz) raspberries

45 ml (3 tbsp) granulated sugar

strawberries and raspberries, to decorate

1 Cut the crusts off the bread and cut the bread slices into neat fingers. Reserve about a quarter and use the rest to line the base and sides of two 150 ml ($\frac{1}{4}$ pint) ramekin dishes, making sure that there are no spaces between the bread.

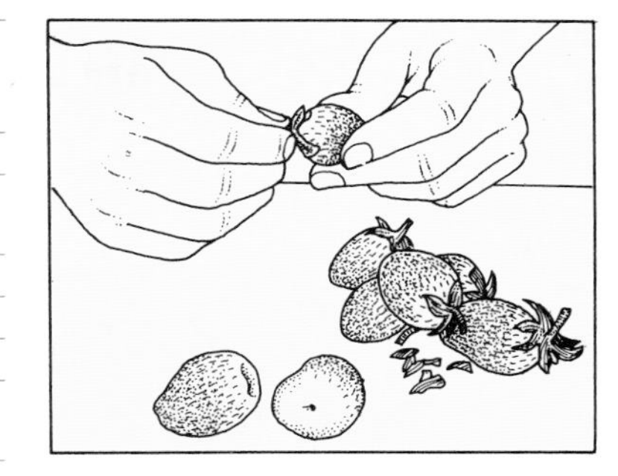

2 Hull the strawberries and put into a medium bowl with the raspberries. Sprinkle with the sugar and add 45 ml (3 tbsp) water. Cover and cook on HIGH for 5–7 minutes or until the sugar dissolves, the juices begin to flow and the fruit softens.

3 Reserve about 45 ml (3 tbsp) of the juice and pour the remaining fruit and juice into the lined ramekins. Cover with the reserved bread.

4 Place a small saucer with a weight on it on top of each pudding and refrigerate overnight.

5 To serve, turn out on to two serving plates and spoon over the reserved juice. Decorate with strawberries and raspberries.

Battenburg Cake

0.45* ⌂ £ ✳* 397–496 cals

* plus 2 hours cooling time; freeze after step 5

Serves 8–10

175 g (6 oz) softened butter or soft tub margarine
175 g (6 oz) caster sugar
a few drops of vanilla flavouring
3 eggs, beaten
175 g (6 oz) self raising flour
30–60 ml (2–4 tbsp) milk
30 ml (2 tbsp) cocoa powder
120 ml (8 tbsp) apricot jam
225 g (8 oz) marzipan
caster sugar, to dredge

1 Grease a shallow 18 × 23 cm (7 × 9 inch) dish. Divide the dish in half lengthways with a 'wall' of greasproof paper. To make a wall of greasproof paper, take a piece about 7.5 cm (3 inches) wider than the cake dish and make a 4 cm ($1\frac{1}{2}$ inch) pleat in the centre. Place in the dish.

2 Put the butter or margarine, caster sugar, vanilla flavouring, eggs, flour and 30 ml (2 tbsp) milk in a bowl and beat until smooth. Alternatively, put the ingredients in a food processor or mixer and mix until smooth.

3 Spoon half the mixture into one side of the prepared dish and level the surface.

4 Add the cocoa powder and a little more milk, if necessary, to the remaining mixture to make a very soft dropping consistency. Spoon this into the other side of the prepared dish and level the surface. Cook on HIGH for 5–6 minutes or until the cake is well risen, but still looks slightly moist on the surface.

5 Leave to stand for 5 minutes, then carefully turn out and leave to cool on a wire rack.

6 Trim the two sponges to an equal size and cut each in half lengthways.

7 Put the apricot jam in a small bowl and cook on HIGH for $1\frac{1}{2}$–2 minutes or until hot, stirring frequently. Spread one side of one piece of the vanilla sponge with apricot jam and then place one piece of the chocolate sponge next to it and press the two firmly together.

8 Spread more jam on top of the two halves and place the remaining two sponges on top, alternating the colours.

9 Roll out the marzipan to an oblong long enough to go around the sponge cakes. Brush the marzipan with apricot jam and place the sponge cakes in the centre. Bring the marzipan up over the sides to enclose the sponges, then turn the cake over so the join is underneath.

10 Press the marzipan firmly around the sponges to seal. Trim each end neatly. Use a small knife to decorate the top of the cake with a criss-cross pattern. Pinch the top side edges between thumb and forefinger to give a fluted edge. Dredge lightly with caster sugar and place on a serving dish.

ENGLISH MADELEINES

0.25* £ ✳* 240 cals

* plus 1 hour cooling time; freeze after step 5

Serves 8

100 g (4 oz) softened butter or soft tub margarine

100 g (4 oz) caster sugar

2 eggs

100 g (4 oz) self raising flour

75 ml (5 tbsp) red jam

40 g ($1\frac{1}{2}$ oz) desiccated coconut

4 glacé cherries, halved, and angelica pieces, to decorate

1 Line the bases of eight paper drinking cups with rounds of greaseproof paper.

2 Put the butter, sugar, eggs and flour in a bowl and beat until smooth. Alternatively, put the ingredients in a food processor or mixer and mix until smooth.

3 Divide the mixture evenly between the prepared cups. Place the cups on two flat plates, four on each plate.

4 Cook one plate at a time on HIGH for $1\frac{1}{2}$–2 minutes or until risen, but still slightly moist on the surface. Leave to stand for 1–2 minutes, then turn out and leave to cool on a wire rack.

5 When the cakes are cold, trim the bases, if necessary, so that they stand firmly and are about the same height.

6 Put the jam in a small bowl and cook on HIGH for 1–2 minutes until melted. Stir well.

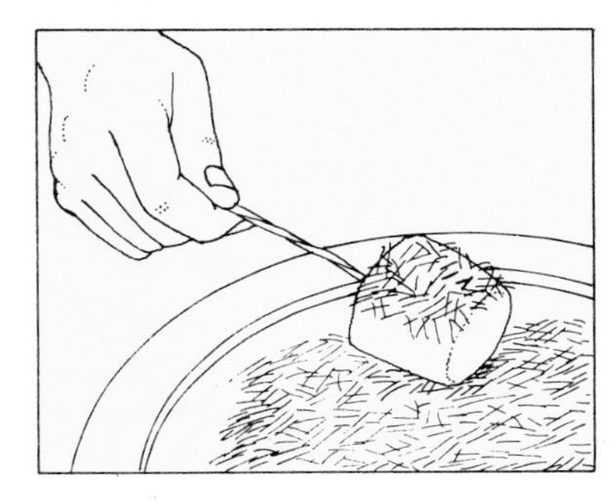

7 Spread the coconut out on a large plate. Spear a cake on a skewer or a fork, brush with the jam and then roll in the coconut until evenly coated. Repeat with the remaining cakes.

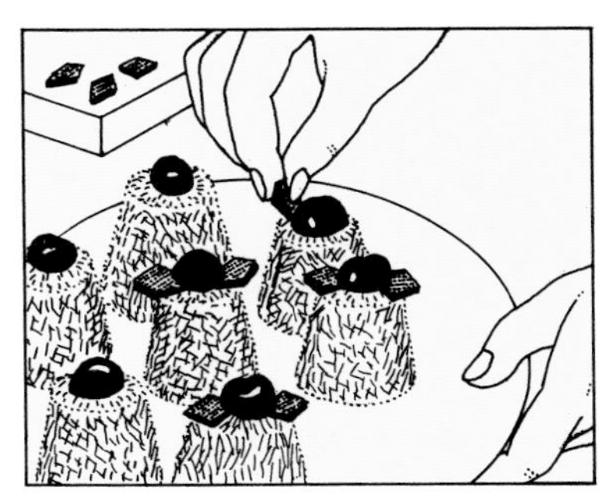

8 Top each Madeleine with half a glacé cherry and small pieces of angelica. These cakes are best eaten on the day of making.

CHOCOLATE PRALINE CAKE

0.30* £ £ ✱* 666 cals

* plus 2 hours cooling time; freeze after step 6

Serves 8

175 g (6 oz) blanched almonds

275 g (10 oz) caster sugar

100 g (4 oz) softened butter or soft tub margarine

2 eggs

45 ml (3 tbsp) clear honey

150 ml ($\frac{1}{4}$ pint) soured cream

100 g (4 oz) self raising flour

40 g ($1\frac{1}{2}$ oz) cocoa powder

50 g (2 oz) ground almonds

300 ml ($\frac{1}{2}$ pint) whipping cream

1 To make the praline, grease a baking sheet and set aside. Spread out the almonds on a large ovenproof plate and cook on HIGH for 4–5 minutes until lightly browned, stirring frequently.

2 Put 175 g (6 oz) of the sugar in a large heatproof bowl with 60 ml (4 tbsp) water and cook on HIGH for 3 minutes. Stir until the sugar has dissolved, then continue to cook on HIGH for 5–7 minutes until the sugar is golden brown. Turn the bowl occasionally but do not stir. Add the nuts and stir until coated.

3 Pour the praline on to the baking sheet and leave for 10–15 minutes to cool and harden.

4 Meanwhile, make the cake. Grease a 1.6 litre ($2\frac{3}{4}$ pint) ring mould and set aside.

5 Put the butter or margarine and remaining sugar in a bowl and beat together until pale and fluffy. Gradually beat in the eggs, honey and soured cream. Fold in the flour, cocoa and ground almonds.

6 Spoon the cake mixture into the prepared dish. Stand on a roasting rack and cook on HIGH for 10 minutes until risen but still slightly moist on the surface. Leave to stand for 5 minutes, then turn out on to a wire rack to cool.

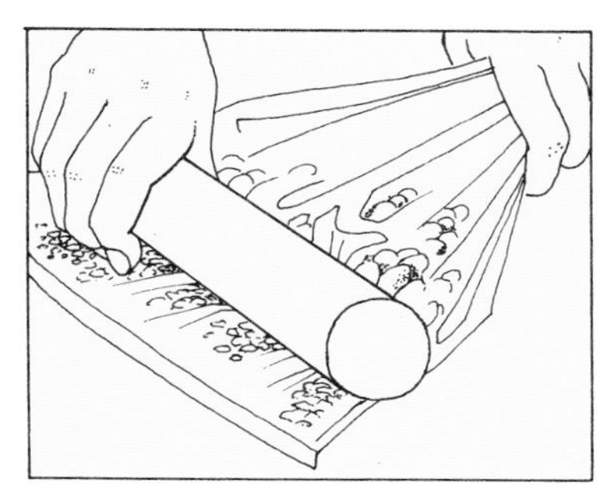

7 While the cake is cooling, coarsely crush half the praline with a rolling pin in a strong polythene bag. Finely crush the remaining praline in a coffee grinder or food processor.

8 Whip the cream until stiff, then gradually fold in the finely crushed praline. Spread the cream on to the cake to coat it completely. Sprinkle with the coarsely crushed praline.

PRALINE

When making the praline, it is important to dissolve the sugar completely, before cooking to a light golden colour, to prevent it from crystallizing. Likewise, once the sugar has dissolved, do not stir but turn the bowl, in case your cooker has a hot spot.

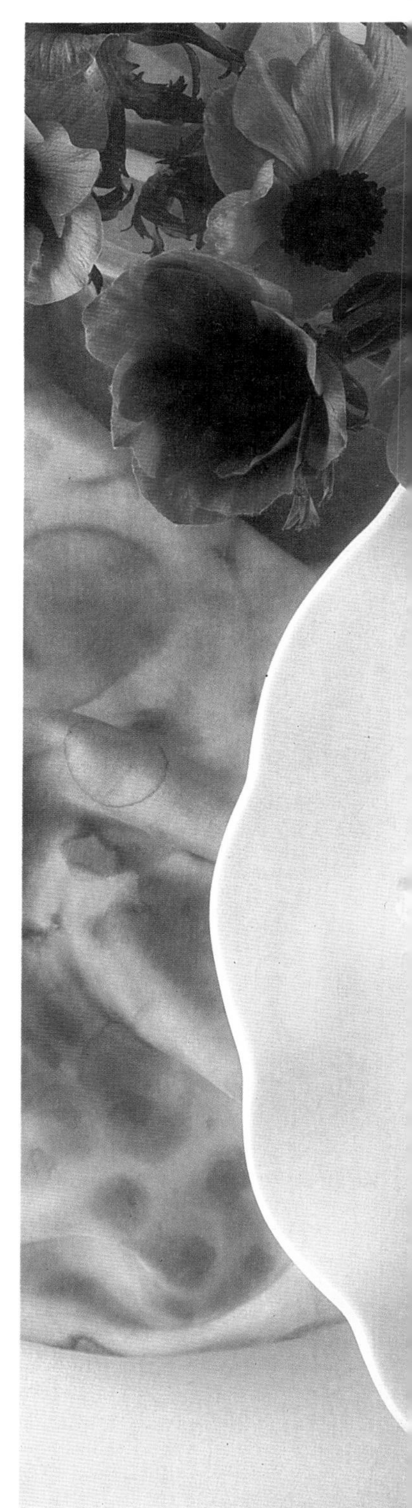

FLAPJACKS

0.05* | 62 cals

* plus 1 hour cooling

Makes 16

75 g (3 oz) butter or margarine

50 g (2 oz) light soft brown sugar

30 ml (2 tbsp) golden syrup

175 g (6 oz) porridge oats

1 Grease a shallow 12.5 × 23 cm (5 × 9 inch) dish. Put the butter or margarine, sugar and syrup in a large bowl. Cook on HIGH for 2 minutes until the sugar has dissolved, stirring once. Stir well, then mix in the oats.

2 Press the mixture into the dish. Stand on a roasting rack and cook on HIGH for 2–3 minutes until firm to the touch.

3 Leave to cool slightly, then mark into sixteen bars. Allow to cool completely before turning out of the dish.

FLAPJACKS

Few biscuits are suitable for cooking in a microwave because they can only be cooked in small batches and often need to be turned over. These flapjacks, however, are one of the quickest and easiest biscuits to make in the microwave.

WALNUT, BANANA AND ORANGE TEABREAD

0.20* £ ✳ 209 cals

* plus 1 hour cooling

Makes 16 slices

225 g (8 oz) self raising wholemeal flour

100 g (4 oz) light soft brown sugar

100 g (4 oz) butter or margarine

100 g (4 oz) walnut halves, roughly chopped

3 ripe bananas, mashed

1 egg

finely grated rind and juice of 1 large orange

2.5 ml ($\frac{1}{2}$ tsp) ground mixed spice

For the topping

25 g (1 oz) walnut halves

25 g (1 oz) dried banana chips

15 ml (1 tbsp) clear honey

1 Grease a 1.7 litre (3 pint) loaf dish. Line with greaseproof paper and grease the paper.

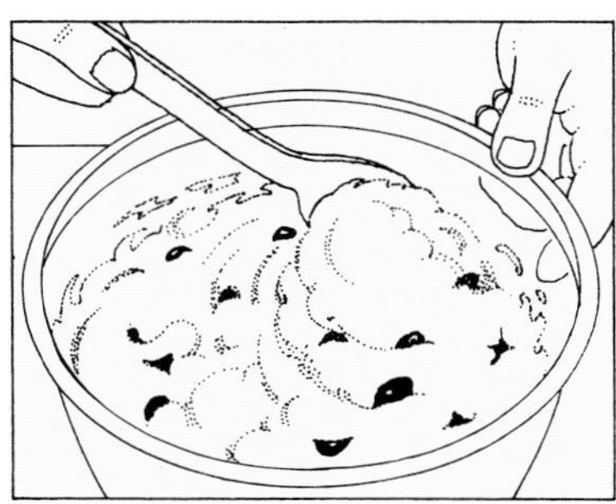

2 Put the flour, sugar, butter, walnuts, bananas, egg, orange rind and juice and mixed spice in a large bowl and beat thoroughly until well mixed.

3 Spoon the mixture into the prepared dish and level the surface. Sprinkle with the walnuts and banana chips for the topping. Stand on a roasting rack and cook on MEDIUM for 14 minutes until risen and firm to the touch.

4 Leave to cool in the dish. When cold turn out and brush with the honey to glaze. Serve sliced, plain or spread with a little butter or margarine. Walnut, Banana and Orange Teabread will keep wrapped in foil for 1–2 days.

GRIDDLE SCONES

0.20 ✳ 260 cals

Makes 8

225 g (8 oz) self raising flour

2.5 ml ($\frac{1}{2}$ tsp) salt

15 g ($\frac{1}{2}$ oz) butter or margarine

25 g (1 oz) caster sugar

about 150 ml ($\frac{1}{4}$ pint) milk or buttermilk

butter and jam, for serving

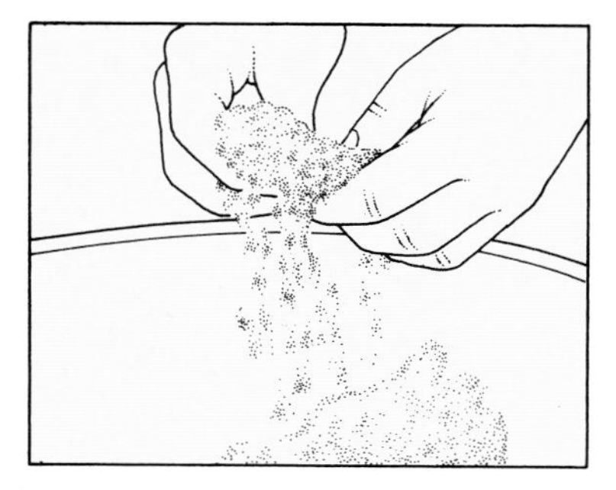

1 Put the flour and salt in a bowl. Using both hands, rub in the butter or margarine until the mixture resembles fine breadcrumbs, then stir in the sugar. Add enough milk or buttermilk to give a soft but manageable dough.

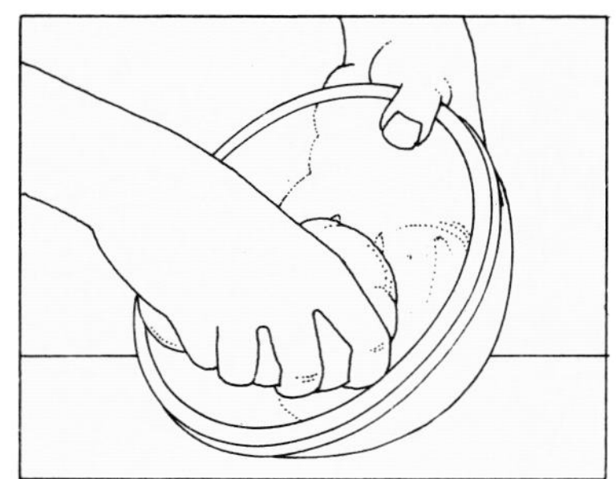

2 With one hand, collect the mixture together and knead lightly for a few seconds to give a firm, smooth dough. Divide in two and roll into two rounds 0.5 cm ($\frac{1}{4}$ inch) thick. Cut each round into four.

3 Heat a large browning dish, skillet or griddle on HIGH for 4–5 minutes. Do not allow the dish to become too hot or the scones will burn.

4 Quickly place four quarters on the browning dish and cook on HIGH for $1\frac{1}{2}$ minutes. Turn the scones over and cook on HIGH for a further 2 minutes. Repeat with the remaining scones, without reheating the browning dish. Eat while still hot, spread with butter.

GRIDDLE SCONES

A microwave browning dish, skillet or griddle gives perfectly browned scones just like a conventional griddle. They are made of a material which can withstand a very high temperature and are heated empty before the food to be cooked is placed on the hot surface. This immediately sears and browns the food. Manufacturers usually recommend that they are heated on HIGH for 5–8 minutes but for this recipe it should only be heated for 4–5 minutes otherwise it will become too hot and the scones will burn.

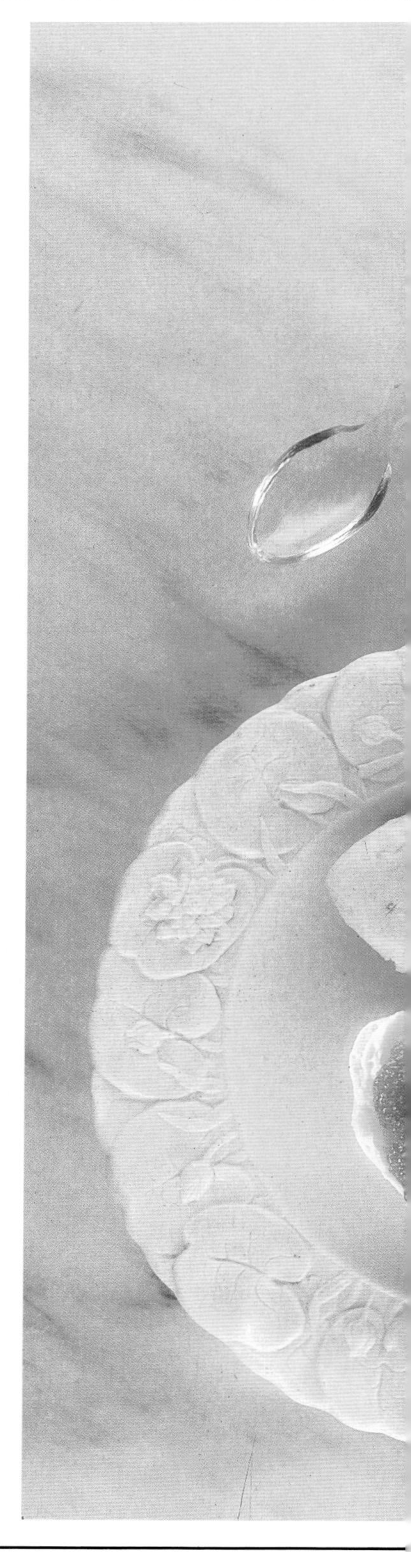

INDEX

GOOD HOUSEKEEPING

...For the life women REALLY lead

Dear Reader,

We do hope you will enjoy your **Good Housekeeping** cookery book and will go on to collect the other titles available from your **BP Service Station.** Each recipe given has been double tested for success by our highly respected and unique resource, the **Good Housekeeping Institute,** so you can try new dishes with complete confidence.

It is that same confidence and trust that makes millions of women read our **Good Housekeeping** magazine each month. Colourful and glossy, it is always brimming over with new and exciting ideas, plus practical advice on a huge range of topics that affect all our everyday lives. No wonder so many people now subscribe to **Good Housekeeping** each month to ensure they don't miss a single copy.

Uniquely for BP customers we are offering a special introductory rate to all new UK subscribers of only £11.20 – *a saving of £2 on the current rate!* For this amount you will receive a copy of Good Housekeeping by post each month for 12 months.

Credit card holders can order by telephoning 0444 440421 or by post to the address below.

Happy reading!

Brian Braithwaite
Publishing Director – Good Housekeeping

Subscription enquiries and orders with payment to:
Quadrant Subscription Services, FREEPOST, Haywards Heath, West Sussex RH16 3ZA.
Offer closes 31st August 1989.

IMPORTANT: TO QUALIFY FOR YOUR DISCOUNT QUOTE "SAK" IN ALL COMMUNICATIONS.

Published by Ebury Press
Division of The National Magazine Company Ltd
Colquhoun House
27–37 Broadwick Street
London W1V 1FR

The Good Housekeeping Institute is the food and consumer research centre of Good Housekeeping magazine.
Printed and bound in Italy by New Interlitho, S.p.a., Milan